Although the author has taken all reasonable care in preparing this book, we make no warranty about the accuracy or completeness of its content and, to the maximum extent permitted, the author assumes no liability for accidents happening to, or injuries sustained by, readers who engage in the activities described in this book. Hang safe!

There are several QR codes you can scan throughout this book that link to additional resources. You'll need a QR reader for your mobile device to use.

Get a free QR reader from http://scan.mobi

ISBN-13: 978-1466263680

ISBN-10: 1466263687

Library of Congress Control Number: 2011917638

10 9 8 7 6 5 4 3

First edition published November 2011. Revised February 2012.

TABLE OF CONTENTS

New to hammock camping? Start here!

"Simply amazing! If you are new to hammock camping, already love hammock camping, or just simply want to spread the word, this book is a must have."
—*Adam Hurst, HammockGear.com*

"If you want to invigorate your backpacking experience and sleep consistently in or on any terrain then this book will give you all the gathered intel on the wonders of hanging cradled in comfort. Hammock camping is a former tarp-only campers dream. Hammock camping has a learning curve and is not for everyone...but if you are ready for a new level of wonder in the backwoods then this book will be you guide. It is truly a right goodie!"
—*Sean "Shug" Emery*

"A fast, interesting, and excellent read. The illustrations really add to both reading enjoyment and clarity. Hammock camping has steadily evolved over the last decade as a comfortable, sustainable, low-impact camping lifestyle. *The Ultimate Hang* will enhance the hammock hanging experience of novice and veteran hangers alike."
—*Jack Tier and Jack Myers,*
Owners and founders of Jacks 'R' Better, LLC

"Finally, a modern-day, comprehensive resource on all aspects of hammock camping. The lighthearted illustrations along with excellent explanations make for a quick and enjoyable read. Every current and future hammock user should have this on their bookshelf."
—*Stuart Raike, whoopieslings.com*

"Derek's book demonstrates the basic principles as well as the more advanced techniques of hammock camping in one easy-to-understand compendium. Not only does *The Ultimate Hang* cover the ins and outs of hammock camping, it also explores some of the gear currently being offered by hammock retailers and its use.
Even someone like me, who has been using hammocks for years, learned a thing or two from *The Ultimate Hang*. This is a must-have book for those just starting out in the world of hammock camping or long time users such as myself."
— *Jason "Headchange4u" Turner*

ACKNOWLEDGEMENTS

I wish to express my gratitude to my family, especially my wife, who allowed me to go on so many hikes and backpacking trips where I tested and explored hammock camping. I also credit my wife for encouraging me to write and illustrate this book and her assistance in editing, and for the many nights when I bored her to sleep with long, tedious one-sided conversations about hammocks. I am also grateful to my brothers, Cameron, Jason, and Breton for their input and editing skills, and my wonderful parents, who helped edit early drafts and who have always begged me to illustrate a book.

To my friend Bill Linney I owe many thanks for his late night reviews and publishing acumen that helped make this project successful.

I'd like to extend specific appreciation to friends and forum members:

"Just Jeff" Jackson	Jason "Headchange4u" Turner
Tim "slowhike" Garner	Mike "te-wa" Stivers
Sean "Shug" Emery	Thom "Dutch" Ressler
Jack Myers	Jack Tier
Grant "Cannibal" Doner	Patrick "NCPatrick" Brown
Sam "Angry Sparrow" Lentz	Stuart Raike
Adam "Stormcrow" Hurst	Paul Gibson

...and to various hammock manufacturers for reviewing the manuscript and making valuable suggestions and corrections.

This book represents a collection of my own experiences and trials, but it also benefits from feedback and the giving spirit of members on HammockForums.net who constantly innovate, explore, and experiment with hammock camping.

—Derek

Simplicity is the ultimate sophistication.
—Leonardo da Vinci

INTRODUCTION

No worries!

My first experience in an all-in-one camping hammock was with an Expedition ASYM from Hennessy Hammock. It was summertime in Virginia and the Asian tiger mosquitoes were at their peak. I jumped in the hammock and escaped the blood-sucking rascals, thanks to its protective sewn-in bug netting. I didn't worry about the light drizzle coming down because the hammock came with a matching rain fly. I adjusted my position inside to find the "sweet spot" by laying in a diagonal line. Within moments I was relaxing in recumbent bliss.

When I sleep on the ground or even on my bed at home, I toss and turn when my back, arms, or shoulders get uncomfortable. In contrast, the hammock removed most, if not all, the pressure points naturally. I was so comfortable I slept the entire night on my back without moving much. I woke refreshed with an added bonus: no bug bites!

Beyond the comfort, I loved the hammock because it was suspended a few feet above the ground, away from protruding pebbles, soggy soil, crawling critters, and insect infestations. This also meant that getting out of this new "tent" was as easy as standing up.

No more crawling and squirming into small spaces, no more drying my tent out before packing, and no more scraping off muck, leaves, and slugs.

I raved about hammocks to family and friends, describing how it was like "sleeping on a cloud" and vowed never to sleep on the ground again.

However, since that first "hang," I've had my share of disappointments. When the temperature dropped, I discovered "cold butt syndrome" (CBS) and learned that my sleeping bag alone wasn't enough to keep me warm. I struggled through the winter experimenting with different insulation options, and only those first summer sleeps encouraged me to stick with it.

I learned a thing or two after that first winter and I now stay warm, dry, and insect-free year-round! Today, innovations in insulation and other conveniences have allowed manufacturers to take hammock camping more mainstream, meaning more people are discovering the comfort, practicality, and protection from sleeping above the ground, without experiencing their own "trial by ice."

With so many styles of hammocks, so many techniques for anchoring a hammock, and so much variety in staying warm, dry, and bug free, it can be difficult to find what works best for you. This book provides fresh ideas, standard practices, and reliable resources to give you the ultimate hang, whether you are new to hammock camping or are an experienced hanger.

HAMMOCK CAMPING: A HISTORY, ABRIDGED

When I talk to family and friends about hammock camping, I often hear, "I can *nap* in a hammock, but *sleep all night?* Isn't that *uncomfortable?*" As I probe further, I find these doubters have a modern concept of hammocks linked to the spreader bar hammock so common in many backyards. Spreader bar hammocks take the original design and try to flatten it out like a bed by using long bars on each end. This design raises the center of gravity, creating a very tippy bed. In addition, the large mesh weave becomes uncomfortable over time, making these hammocks usable for only short durations.

So, where did hammocks come from and what were they like? Most sources point to the first nations in South America as the inventors of the hammock[1]. These elevated beds were woven from the bark of trees and gathered at the ends. They hung loose and deep in the middle, creating a low center of gravity and a secure, non-tipping "nest." By sleeping at an angle to the center line (i.e., diagonally)—the "Brazilian" way, as it is called—the occupant slept ergonomically flat, not dramatically curved from head to toe.

The benefits of sleeping in a hammock were clear: better sanitation; a cooler, more comfortable sleep; less infection; and less interaction with biting insects and poisonous snakes.

The hammock was one of the first discoveries that influenced Christopher Columbus[2] upon landing in the Americas in 1492. Columbus is credited with exporting the hammock to Europe where it was eventually adopted as the standard bunk in sailing ships for hundreds of years[3].

Outside of ships and the indigenous people of South America, hammock camping was slower to adopt *en masse*. Sir Robert Baden-Powell[4] recorded using a hammock tent in the late 1800s and promoted sleeping above the ground to the Boy Scouts in 1907. Scientists and explorers who visited Central and South America in the 1900s also recognized the benefits of hammocks. They used the

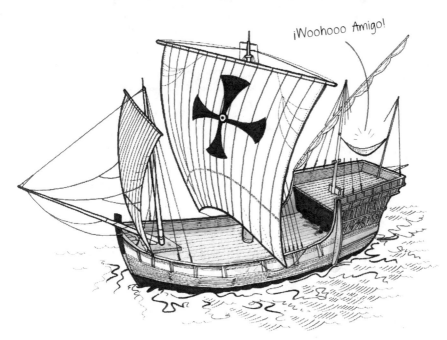

¡Woohooo Amigo!

Venezuelan hammock, with its highly-breathable woven fabric. This style was modified by adding a tarp, bug netting, and drip lines. This design became known as the "jungle" hammock.

With input from Maj. Cresson Kearny[5], the U.S. military commissioned their own versions of the jungle hammock, for the Allied Forces in World War II and later in Vietnam. These nylon hammocks were the inspiration for modern designs by Tom Hennessy (Hennessy Hammock) and Gary Clark (Clark Jungle Hammock), who offer some popular commercial camping hammocks today.

Hammock camping has grown in popularity with backpackers looking for lightweight, comfortable shelters, especially during the peak summer season; yet hangers have long wanted to use them in colder climates. Innovators like Ed Speer (Speer Hammock), Jack Tier and Jack Myers (Jacks 'R' Better), Sgt. Rock, Dave Womble, Tom Hennessy, and Brandon Waddy (Warbonnet Outdoors), were some of the first to introduce hammock-specific insulation options that made hammock camping possible year-round.

Today we are lucky to have dozens of manufacturers who specialize in hammock camping gear.

NOTES
1. "Hammock." (n.d.) http://en.wikipedia.org/wiki/Hammock
2. "What Came To Be Called America." (n.d.) http://www.loc.gov/exhibits/1492/america.html
3. David Phillipson, *Roll on the Rodney!* (1999) cited in http://www.independent.co.uk
4. Baden-Powell, *Young Knights of the Empire*, (1916), 184
5. "Cresson Kearney" (n.d.) http://en.wikipedia.org/wiki/Cresson_Kearny

HAMMOCK CAMPING OVERVIEW

Camping hammocks are so named because they use quick-drying, mildew-resistant fabrics, and integrate standard outdoor protections like bug netting and a waterproof rain fly. In other words, all the protections of a tent, only roomier, lighter, easier to maintain, more customizable, and above all else, **built-in comfort you can look forward to night after night.**

You can use gear you already own to start camping in a hammock today! Items like sleeping bags and insulating pads are still used in hammocks, although you may have to make a few adjustments. There is, however, specific hammock camping gear that you don't often find with tents, like climbing hardware, tree straps, suspension ropes, and "under quilts."

People who gravitate to hammock camping tend to tinker and experiment. Some have introduced new techniques or borrowed materials from other industries that have made it easier to hang a hammock or significantly reduce its weight and bulk. A basic hammock is also so simple in its construction that many people make their own or customize it with homemade gear.

You can find camping hammocks complete with integrated, zippered bug netting and a matching rain fly ready to go out of the box. You can also buy the components separately, something you don't find with tents (don't like the color of that rain fly? Too bad!). I personally like to mix-and-match the parts of my hammock so I can fine-tune my sleep system for different conditions and to personalize the components to my liking. Tent parts, on the other hand, are not usually interchangeable, and some pole structures are too complicated to allow for field repairs. Hammock systems are simple and lightweight so you can bring along a backup set of suspension lines and straps with hardly a penalty in weight or bulk.

LOOKING FOR LIGHTWEIGHT GEAR? You'll find hammocks in every weight category and style to suit your needs. Breakthroughs in lightweight fabrics and other design innovations have made it possible for ultralighters to find comfortable hammock systems and keep a sub-5 lbs. (2.3 kg.) base weight.

HAMMOCKS

TENTS

HAMMOCKS	TENTS
✓ Comfortable	✓ Totally enclosed shelter
✓ Portable (great for day hikes or camping trips)	✓ Great for sharing a shelter with more than one person
✓ Lightweight solo shelter	✓ Great for above the tree line (no extra supports needed) for a free-standing shelter
✓ Quick and easy to set up—nothing touches the ground so everything stays clean and dry	✓ Inherently warmer shelter
✓ A separate rain fly lets you set up out of the rain	✖ Compacts the soil
✓ Sleep above bugs and slimy stuff	✖ Heavy and bulky
✓ Quick drying synthetic fabrics	✖ Can get hot and muggy
✓ No rocks, roots, or twigs in your back	✖ Can slide and shift if not on a level spot
✓ Leave No Trace friendly: no compacting the soil, no need to alter a site	✖ Condensation collector
✓ Personalize and modularize the components	✖ Need to clear the ground of rocks, roots, and twigs
✓ Helps relieve aching muscles and back pain (conforms to your body's shape)	✖ Must find a relatively flat spot to set up
✓ Easy to get up from a sitting position in the morning	✖ Cramped and small
✓ Great for uneven, rough terrain	✖ Have to crawl around inside
✖ Cold without insulation (great for sweltering summer, but a challenge in cooler months)	✖ In a heavily-used site after a rain storm, a tent is prone to flood as water can drain into the shelter
✖ Requires two anchor points to pitch above the ground	✖ Must dry out the shelter, scrape off muck from the bottom, and sweep/shake it out before packing and storing
✖ Requires tweaking for a "flat" sleep	
✖ Not ideal for multiple people	

HAMMOCK CAMPING TERMINOLOGY

Throughout this book I will use some terms that are commonly used among fellow hangers but may be new to you.

(A.) **Anchor**—Attachment point, usually created with non-stretching webbing straps.

Bridge Hammock—A hammock modeled after a suspension bridge, that allows the occupant a flat lay head-to-foot (**see page 46**).

(B.) **Bug Netting**—Fine-meshed fabric screen to protect from flying and biting insects. Can be sewn onto a hammock or wrapped around for 360° protection (**see page 96**).

Cold Butt Syndrome (CBS)—A phenomenon caused by inadequate insulation beneath a hammock, creating cold spots on your back, usually starting with your backside (**see page 85**).

Double Layer—A hammock with two fabric layers where insulation can be wedged in between.

Gathered-end Hammock—A hammock based on the original designs from South America where a rectangular piece of fabric is gathered at the ends and the occupant sleeps diagonally to the center line (**see page 44**).

Group Hang—A gathering of hangers.

(C.) **Guyline**—A small line or rope that holds out the edges of a tarp or hammock.

Hanger—An enlightened hammock camper.

Hanging—The art of pitching or setting up a hammock.

(D.) **Ridgeline**—A line running from the two end points on a hammock or a tarp. Useful for hanging items, lifting a bug net, or preventing a hammock from being pulled too tight or too loose.

(E.) **Suspension Line**—The line running from the hammock to the anchor point.

Winter Tarp—A large tarp with extra tie-outs and side panel "doors" (either sewn on or detachable) to create a fully-enclosed shelter (**see page 76**).

Top Quilt (TQ)—A sleeping bag without a zipper or back that lays on top of the hanger and tucks in the sides like a quilt (**see page 90**).

Under Cover—A waterproof shield to protect a hammock and under quilt from splashes (**see page 77**).

F. **Under Quilt** (UQ)—Insulation wrapped underneath a hammock to avoid being compressed (**see page 88**).

The Ultimate Hang—Getting a hammock pitched near a breath-taking vista.

Whoopie Slings—A lightweight, low-bulk, adjustable suspension line made of high-strength Dyneema cord (**see page 56**).

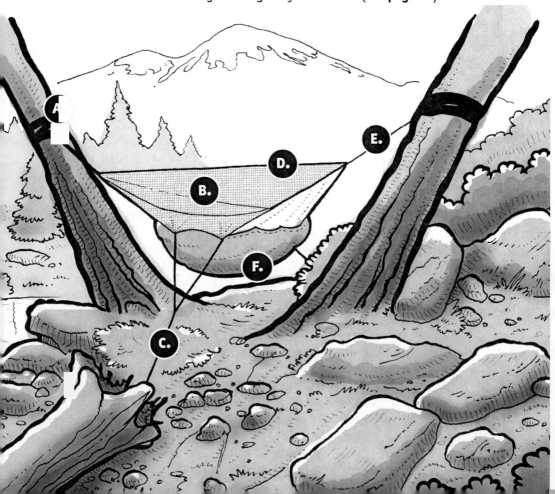

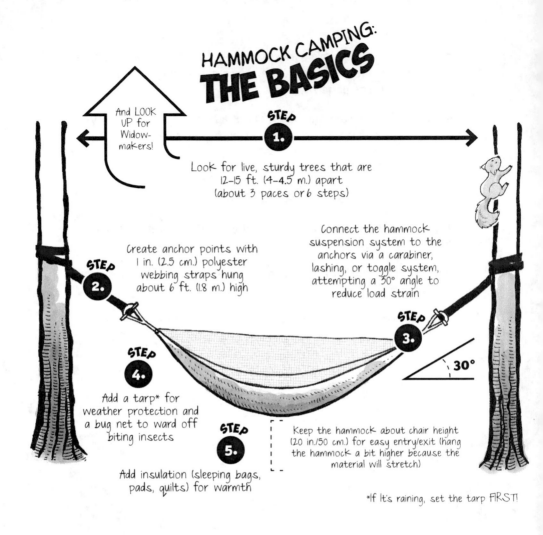

HAMMOCK CAMPING:
THE BASICS

And LOOK UP for Widow-makers!

STEP 1.
Look for live, sturdy trees that are 12-15 ft. (4-4.5 m.) apart (about 3 paces or 6 steps)

STEP 2.
Create anchor points with 1 in. (2.5 cm.) polyester webbing straps hung about 6 ft. (1.8 m.) high

Connect the hammock suspension system to the anchors via a carabiner, lashing, or toggle system, attempting a 30° angle to reduce load strain

STEP 3.
30°

STEP 4.
Add a tarp* for weather protection and a bug net to ward off biting insects

STEP 5.
Add insulation (sleeping bags, pads, quilts) for warmth

Keep the hammock about chair height (20 in./50 cm.) for easy entry/exit (hang the hammock a bit higher because the material will stretch)

*If It's raining, set the tarp FIRST!

Whether you're setting up your hammock for the first time or you've got a few hangs under your belt, It's a good idea to refresh the basics. We'll address each topic in depth later in the book, but these quick pointers should get you laying in the right direction.

Stringing up a hammock is simple, and when done right, it not only improves your comfort, but protects outdoor resources and reduces equipment failure. These basic principles are not hard and fast rules. Understand the basics and adapt the principles for your hammock and the conditions.

If you're new to hammock camping, review this section and practice the basics before diving too deep into this book.

BASIC GEAR NEEDED

- ◆ Hammock
- ◆ Tree Straps
- ◆ Suspension Line
- ◆ Rain Tarp
- ◆ Bug Netting
- ◆ Insulation

An all-in-one camping hammock (e.g., Hennessy Hammock, Warbonnet Outdoors, Clark Jungle Hammock, etc.) will integrate most of these items together, just like a tent, but you can also piece together these items to your liking. To be viable in the outdoors your hammock will need weather protection, adequate insulation, and bug protection depending on the season. Tree straps and suspension lines are essential items that are often overlooked. **Some hammock manufacturers sell only the hammock body, so be sure you have a way to tie up or "suspend" the hammock and anchor it safely, securely, and in a manner that does not damage trees.**

See page 44 for more information on hammock styles.

THE HAMMOCK—Most camping hammocks are gathered at the ends and are roughly the same size: between 9–10 ft. (2.5–3 m.) long and 4–5 ft. (1–1.5 m.) wide. The recommendations in this book are tailored for camping hammocks and will work in nearly all situations. Using these techniques will ensure you have the right distance and space for rain protection, straps, and suspension lines.

STEP 1: THE PERFECT TREES

Hammock Physics? See page 24. What's a pace? See page 41.

The first thing to look for are anchor points that are between 12–15 ft. (4–5 m.) apart. If you're using trees, they should be at least 6 in. (15 cm.) in diameter—thick and strong enough to hold your weight but not too big to wrap your straps. Anchor points can be any thing strong enough to support the physics of the hang. I've found perfect spaces in gazebos, pavilions, soccer goal posts, and even between vehicles.

STEP 2: ANCHOR POINTS

Non-stretching polyester webbing straps that are
1-2 in. (2.5–5 cm.) wide work best for creating anchor
points around trees because they help distribute the
weight without cutting into the bark. Loops that are
sewn or tied on the webbing make the process easier.

Learn how to adjust tree straps on page 55.

CAUTION: Avoid tying rope around a tree. You
risk cutting the bark and damaging the nutrient-
rich layers, thus weakening the tree and making it
vulnerable to insects and disease.

To set your straps, reach about head-level (roughly
6 ft./1.8 m. high or higher) and wrap the straps around
the tree to create an anchor point. You can wrap the
webbing multiple times to adjust the length.

Use low-stretch polyester webbing

STEP 3: SUSPENSION LINES

Attach the suspension line to the anchor point using
climbing-grade carabiners or other hardware options.

How do you ensure a perfect sag? See page 43.

You want to make sure the hammock is centered
between the anchor points and at the same relative
height on uneven terrain. This allows hammocks to be
set up in areas where tents would not work. When you
get in the hammock, it should come to rest at about
chair height (20 in./50 cm.). You may need to set the
hammock a few inches higher if the material stretches.

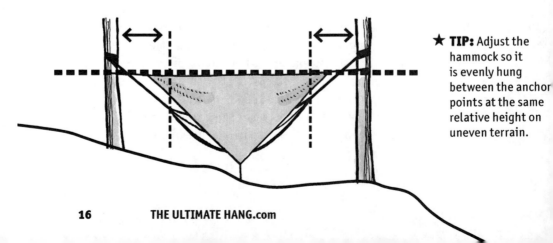

★ **TIP:** Adjust the
hammock so it
is evenly hung
between the anchor
points at the same
relative height on
uneven terrain.

What kinds of tarps offer the most protection? See page 75.

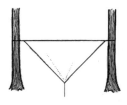

Tree strap with climbing carabiner attached

STEP 4: WEATHER & BUG PROTECTION

A tarp is used for weather protection and bug netting for insect protection. You can use any kind of tarp for a hammock as long as it is big enough to cover you and your gear. An 8 × 8 ft, (2.4 × 2.4 m.) tarp, turned to 45°, makes an excellent diamond shape. Lightweight backpacking tarps designed and sewn specifically for hammocks are available from gear manufacturers. Some hammocks come equipped with sewn-in bug netting that makes setup easier. After-market bug netting is available to fit most hammocks.

An 8×8 ft. (2.4×2.4 m.) tarp in a diamond pitch

SIDE VIEW   **TOP VIEW**   **ISOMETRIC VIEW**

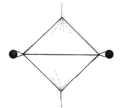
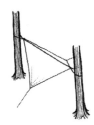

STEP 5: STAYING WARM

To sleep through the night, you'll need some insulation, especially when temperatures drop below 70°F (21°C). A regular sleeping bag will keep you warm on top, but you'll need insulation beneath to stay comfortable. When you lay in a sleeping bag—in a hammock or on the ground—the insulation gets compressed beneath you, rendering it useless. This is why pads are used in tents—in part for comfort, but more to prevent *conductive* heat loss. In a hammock, you'll have *convective* heat loss from the air circulating around you. Laying on a pad inside the hammock will keep you warm (you'll want a wide pad that can wrap around your shoulders too). Most hangers use a

See more ways to stay warm in a hammock on page 84.

sleeping bag or quilt inside and an under quilt beneath to stay warm. There's a lot more information about staying warm on **page 84**.

Some camping hammocks are constructed with two layers of fabric, creating a sleeve where a pad can be secured to keep it from shifting.

GETTING IN AND GETTING COZY

To enter a hammock, spread the fabric wide, take a small step back, and sit down in the center. Swing your legs in and adjust your body so you lay on the diagonal (the Brazilian way) and not in line with the hammock suspension. By laying on the diagonal, you can achieve a nearly flat, ergonomic position in an gathered-end hammock. Move around until you find a "sweet spot" where you drop in place.

Side sleeper? See page 104 (other comfort tips start on page 102).

Typically, a larger, wider hammock is more comfortable than a narrow one. Adjusting the height, hang angle, and anchor distance all have an effect on the lay.

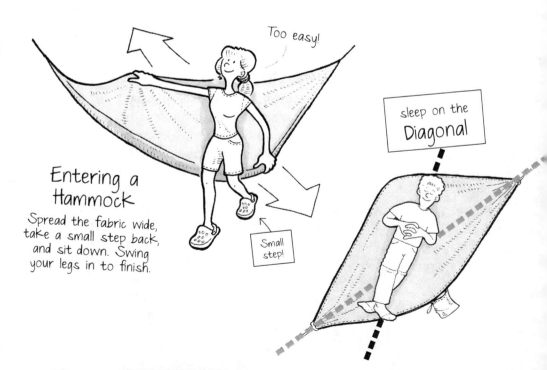

Too easy!

Entering a Hammock

Spread the fabric wide, take a small step back, and sit down. Swing your legs in to finish.

Small step!

sleep on the **Diagonal**

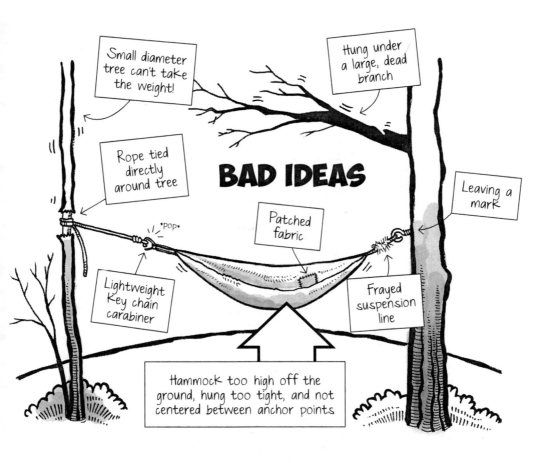

For all the good examples of how to hang, there are plenty of bad ones to lead you astray. Unfortunately, there are some prominent examples showing hammocks tied with rope directly to trees or hung too tight. Sometimes a bad hang will only lead to an uncomfortable sleep, but others may be more hazardous. I've seen people attach mini carabiners to anchor points (yes, they bend and pop off quickly), and even seen hammocks ripped in half because they were strung too tightly.

Hopefully the examples and techniques illustrated in this book will point you in the right direction so you can safely and responsibly enjoy the comfort, convenience, and simplicity of hammock camping.

BREAKING IT DOWN

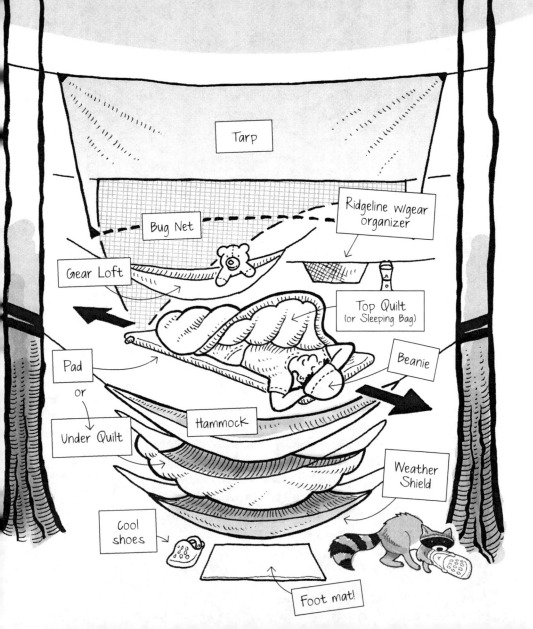

Using a hammock for camping opens up a wide-range of possibilities not available to tents or bivvies. I've pitched hammocks over boulders in Hawaii, across ancient lava flows in Northern Arizona, near cliffs and sloping hills in Virginia, and straddling cacti in Southern Utah. I no longer have to clear the ground of sticks, or rocks, or worry about mud, slugs, and sandy ground (Leave No Trace friendly!). However, although hammocks can be pitched to avoid most obstacles, a good site is still *found*, not *made*. Even with a forest full of trees, it may take a few moments to find a suitable spot.

★ **TIP:** You should rarely, if ever, need to alter a site (e.g., break live tree limbs, remove offending shrubbery) in order to pitch a hammock. In most cases, all you need to do is find another tree.

HANGING SAFE

While a hammock can be pitched just about anywhere, be sensible and assess the risks to determine what location is safe. Hanging over a body of water or near a cliff edge can be an invigorating rush for some, but the risks are high. Even hanging over a pile of jagged rocks or a cactus plant poses potential problems. The major risks with hammocks include unsafe gear, lightning, bears and other animals, and widowmakers.

SAFE AND RELIABLE GEAR

The first consideration to a safe hang is to ensure all parts of your hammock system are safety rated for the weight that will be supported. Most hangers recommend a minimum breaking strength of 250 lbs. (113 kg.) for the hammock fabric itself, and greater

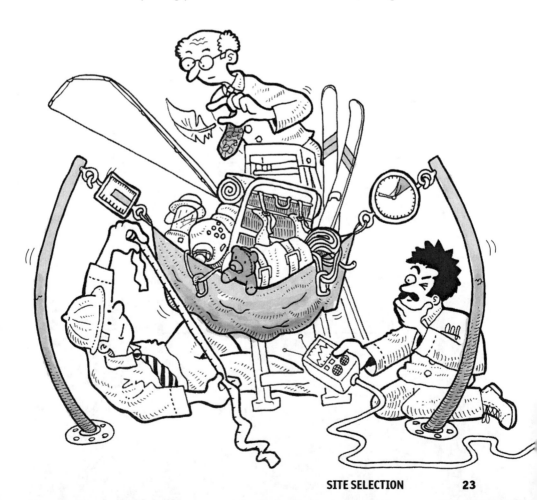

WILL IT HOLD?
(OR, HAMMOCK PHYSICS 101)*

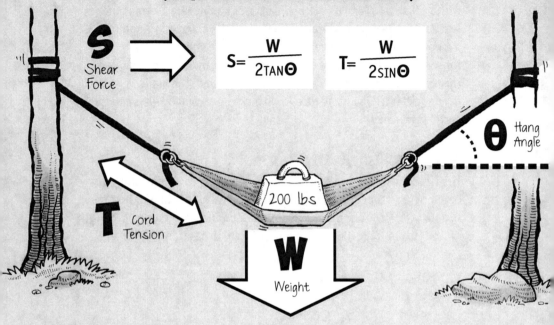

$$S = \frac{W}{2\tan\Theta}$$

$$T = \frac{W}{2\sin\Theta}$$

S Shear Force

T Cord Tension

θ Hang Angle

200 lbs

W Weight

HORIZONTAL (SHEAR) FORCE ON TREES

		Weight *(in pounds, rounded up)*				
		125	**150**	**175**	**200**	**225**	**250**
Hang Angle	**5°**	715	857	1000	1143	1286	1429
	15°	233	280	327	373	420	467
	20°	172	206	240	275	309	344
	30°	108	130	152	173	195	217

Too Tight!

TENSILE FORCE ON ROPES

		Weight *(in pounds, rounded up)*				
		125	**150**	**175**	**200**	**225**	**250**
Hang Angle	**5°**	717	861	1004	1148	1291	1434
	15°	242	270	338	386	435	483
	20°	183	219	256	292	329	366
	30°	125	150	175	200	225	250

Scan this QR code for an interactive hammock hang calculator.

*Calculations used by permission from Jack Myers of Jacks 'R' Better

than 1,000 lbs. (454 kg.) for suspension lines and webbing straps. Your hammock will only be as strong as the weakest link. Falling on the ground because something failed is not a pleasant experience.

In many ways, each component of the hammock should be selected as carefully as climbing and rappelling equipment. Ensure the straps, suspension lines, hardware, and fabric are all in top shape. Any elements showing signs of wear should be properly repaired (if possible) or replaced. It's a good idea to inspect your gear before and after each hang.

When experimenting or testing different techniques, (for example, trying a descender ring with webbing straps) put gear in your hammock to simulate a weight load before sitting in it yourself. Knots should be tied correctly and securely.

Just as a rock climber learns to trust her gear, you will find where your gear feels most secure and where it can take you. Never take it for granted.

LIGHTNING SAFETY

Are hammocks safer in a thunderstorm than tents? Will lightning avoid a hammock since It's elevated above the ground? Electrical storms are a concern for all outdoor activities and hammocks are no exception. Lightning will often follow the path of least resistance, and electricity can flow into a hammock (or tent, for that matter—nylon is no shield against a strike!). Ropes and straps are no defense or protection against lightning.

Although there is no defense for the occasional "out-of-the-blue" strike, *lightning is a manageable risk*. Follow these general rules to minimize getting struck:

◆ Pick a spot to hang in a low stand of trees
◆ Avoid lone or tall trees or isolated groupings
◆ Stay off mountain ridges and hills
◆ Wait at least 30 minutes after the last lightning strike before pitching or moving your hammock

Getting struck by lightning is very rare. When camping, it is more common to encounter small rodents or a falling tree (widowmaker), but those risks are also manageable and avoidable.

For additional information about outdoor safety during a lightning storm, visit the National Weather Service website:

> http://www.lightningsafety.noaa.gov/outdoors.htm

Scan this QR code for more information on NOAA Outdoor Lightning Safety

Mitigate Lightning Strike Risks

Select a spot in a low stand of trees of similar size. Avoid lone or tall trees or isolated groupings!

BEARS AND OTHER ANIMALS

Another common concern when camping outdoors is dealing with animals, specifically bears. While stories about animals investigating hammocks circulate, such encounters are rare. Critters may stroll right under your hammock with not so much as a sniff. Some people joke that hammocks are "bear burritos," but there is very little evidence that animals, particularly bears, are attracted to hammocks, nor that hammocks are inherently associated with food.

Many animals are attracted by odors. Follow Leave No Trace guidelines and keep all scented items away from your sleeping area. This technique will keep most critters from bothering you. It's recommended to cook far away (200 ft./61 m.) from your hammock and pack a "clean" pair of sleeping clothes to change into when it is time for bed.

Highly-impacted areas that have been associated with food smells, like some shelters along the Appalachian Trail, are magnets for small rodents. Hanging a hammock is a great way to avoid these nuisances. For the curious animal that wanders through camp, it is often best to allow them passage without startling them.

WIDOWMAKERS

The most common camping risk is a silent, deadly danger: the widowmaker. Widowmakers are standing dead trees—or live trees with large, dead branches—that pose a nearby or overhead threat. Every year there are devastating reports of campers getting struck by falling trees or overhead branches.

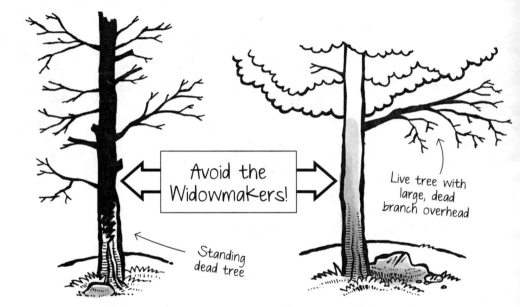

Avoid the Widowmakers!

Standing dead tree

Live tree with large, dead branch overhead

Of all the risks associated with camping, widowmakers are probably the easiest to avoid yet the most overlooked. Standing dead trees are pretty easy to spot (unless you're hanging after dark). Dead trees will be defoliated (no leaves), often missing large sections of bark and branches. Some dead trees will be rotted out and hollow in the center.

Live trees with large, dead branches are a problem because they are less obvious. Be aware of your surroundings and follow these tips to stay clear of widowmakers:

- ◆ Never attach a hammock to a dead tree, no matter how sturdy it seems to you. A strong breeze could topple the tree or send branches falling down.
- ◆ When selecting trees, always **LOOK UP** and make sure the area above you is clear.

WHERE TO HANG

It's like sleeping on a cloud

In a forest full of trees, the abundance of choice can be overwhelming. Instead of looking for a flat area devoid of rocks and roots, you'll be looking for perfectly situated trees near an impressive overlook, or trees close enough together where you and a friend can share a tarp. You may never look at what's on the ground again. For me, there's an irresistible attraction to hang a hammock over large obstacles or above a thicket of thorns, just because I can. I often catch myself thinking, "Oy! That would be a great spot for a hammock!"

Choosing where to hang comes down to picking the right trees in a protected location (away from driving wind and moisture) that offers a great view, without disturbing wildlife and other visitors.

Side-by-Side

A large tarp can cover both hammocks!

Ridgeline with gear organizer

Built-in bug net

Under Quilt

Rock used as guyline stake

PICKING THE RIGHT TREES

The best trees will be alive and offer sturdy trunks or tree limbs—at least 6–8 in. (15–20 cm.) thick— where you can create anchor points with webbing straps. If possible, pick trees with thick, rugged bark, and always bring appropriate straps and padding to protect the bark.

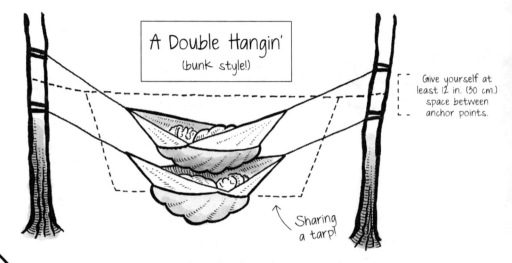

A Double Hangin'
(bunk style!)

Give yourself at least 12 in. (30 cm.) space between anchor points.

Sharing a tarp!

WAIT! WHY TREE STRAPS? This may sound overly protective, but it is for good reason. A single, thin rope can unintentionally cut into the bark, damaging the cambium or nutrient layer of the tree (the life-giving sap of a tree runs through the outer most ring within the bark, not through the center). One hang in an isolated area may never be noticed, but in a popular location with lots of use, small impact grows into a noticeable problem. As more people use hammocks, rangers and camp wardens are keeping note, and in some places, have even made restrictions that limit or prohibit hammock use. Irresponsible individuals can destroy opportunities in the future.

I often backpack with my children and we like to hang our hammocks close together, sharing one tarp for multiple hammocks. To achieve this, finding the right trees that are spaced perfectly is key. With two hammocks in play, I'll usually hang them bunk style, one on top of the other, by pitching the top hammock about a foot (30 cm.) above the lower hammock.

Some trees with strategically-placed limbs can provide multiple anchor points so a few hammocks can be placed close together.

THE LEE SIDE

Keeping clear of wind and precipitation is one step to staying dry and warm. If possible, find a location on the lee side of a hill or outcropping that will provide a pocket of protection. Avoid hilltops that get blasted with wind and are more prone to lightning strikes, and stay out of low valleys where temperature inversions can create significant overnight cold zones (however, these "cold zones" are preferable in the heat of the summer!).

You can find peaceful, protected spots in areas without hills or mountains. Dense vegetation or close groupings of trees can create natural wind breaks and can help deflect sideways rain. Pay attention to the direction of the wind as you hike and take advantage of the topography.

★ **TIP:** Most hammocks can be set up in just a few minutes, meaning you can be more flexible and take time to find a perfect spot.

WIND!

click

Cozy! Protected from the wind

Collect water prior to setting camp

CHOOSE YOUR VIEW

Another advantage of hammocks over ground dwellers is the opportunity to set up in remote locations with unmatched views. Rugged outcroppings and vistas that are difficult or impossible for tents can be perfect for hammocks.

Get away from overly impacted sites *because you can!* It's a great way to reduce "site creep"—an issue at crowded and popular shelters and campgrounds where tent campers progressively spread out an impacted area. Tent campers avoid trampled, muddy areas only to create new ones close by.

If possible, I like to find spots that have many large boulders or rocks near a great view. One of my favorite hangs is on the edge of Walnut Canyon in Northern Arizona. There is literally no place a tent could be pitched with any degree of comfort, so with my hammock I have the entire ledge to myself. Although I was in no danger of falling, I was close enough to the edge to have unobstructed views across the canyon. In the morning, the sun hit the edge of the canyon, lighting up the valley below. A sheen of white mist retreated slowly into a draw, creating a breathtaking scene.

Sweet view!

Stealthy site!

Overcrowded shelter

At least 200 ft. (60 m.) away from the trail and the shelter and water

Take different routes to avoid making new trails

STEALTH HANGING

Sometimes picking the right location is about avoiding other campers and staying out of view. Leave No Trace principles recommend camping at least 200 ft. (60 m.) away from trails, water sources, and other visitors. This is a great way to respect nearby campers, reduce impacting crowded sites, respect wildlife, and enjoy some solitude.

Setting up a hammock site like this is often called "stealth hanging." This technique is part site selection and part gear choice. Look for a site that is well away from overused and highly impacted areas. Pick a site that would be inhospitable to tents. For some, being "stealthy" also means using earth tones or camouflage colored fabrics that easily blend into the surrounding landscape.

Stealth hanging does *not* mean camping illegally. Always be responsible and follow posted rules and policies.

BREAKING IT DOWN
LEAVE NO TRACE

A strong argument for hammock camping is their low-level of impact on the wilderness. By hanging a shelter *above* vegetation (or even better, above rocks or other durable terrain) you eliminate virtually any impact, meaning less compacted soil (plants do not grow well in hard ground). And with the use of tree straps, you can leave a site with no indication that you have ever been there.

But *without* care, even hammocks can cause some damage. There are campgrounds that specifically prohibit hammocks. Often, this is due to a few careless campers, in other cases it is a precautionary tactic due to a location's popularity.

Please adhere to the Seven Principles of Leave No Trace when you are hammock camping.

1. PLAN AHEAD AND PREPARE

Find out ahead of time what is allowed and/or prohibited. Some locations outlaw hammocks or anything tied to trees. Follow any posted rules. The goodwill you spread can go a long way to ensure hammocks are not casually dismissed because of the careless actions of a few.

leave no trace
CENTER FOR OUTDOOR ETHIC

Scan this QR code to learn more about Leave No Trace from LNT.org.

◆ Make sure your webbing straps are long enough to fit the trees you will encounter and at least 1 in. (2.5 cm.) thick to avoid damaging the bark.
◆ Know the regulations and special concerns for the area you'll visit.
◆ Prepare for extreme weather, hazards, and emergencies.
◆ Schedule your trip to avoid times of high use.

Aaah! My tree straps are too short!

- Visit in small groups when possible. Consider splitting larger groups into smaller groups.
- Repackage food to minimize waste.
- Use a map and compass to eliminate the use of marking paint, rock cairns, or flagging.

Durable surfaces!

2. TRAVEL AND CAMP ON DURABLE SURFACES

Since you can hang a hammock over "miserable" terrain, you can often use durable surfaces that can reduce your impact, like rocks, outcroppings, snow, and sand.

While you can find places to hang outside highly-impacted campgrounds, be sure to treat the area as pristine: don't create new trails by walking the same path to and from your hammock. If participating in a group hang in a pristine area, spread out so you limit the impact in any one area.

- Durable surfaces include established trails and campsites, rock, gravel, dry grasses, or snow.
- Protect riparian areas by camping at least 200 ft. (60 m.) from lakes and streams.
- Good campsites are found, not made. Altering a site is not necessary.

- In popular areas:
  - › *Concentrate use on existing trails and campsites.*
  - › *Walk single file in the middle of the trail, even when wet or muddy.*
  - › *Keep campsites small. Focus activity in areas where vegetation is absent.*
- In pristine areas:
  - › *Disperse use to prevent the creation of campsites and trails.*
  - › *Avoid places where impacts are just beginning.*

3. DISPOSE OF WASTE PROPERLY (PACK IT IN, PACK IT OUT)

Some hammock camping kits come with lots of components and there is the possibility for misplacing them. The most common "forgotten" item, according to a poll on HammockForums.net, is a webbing strap (I've had to recover one myself on a backpacking trip). Check your site to ensure you gather all your gear. Some hangers go so far as using brightly colored ribbon, webbing, and guy line to make components easier to find.

- Pack it in, pack it out. Inspect your campsite and rest areas for trash or spilled foods. Pack out all trash, leftover food, and litter.
- Deposit solid human waste in catholes dug 6–8 in. (15–20 cm.) deep at least 200 ft. (60 m.) from water, camp, and trails. Cover and disguise the cathole when finished.
- Pack out toilet paper and hygiene products.
- To wash yourself or your dishes, carry water 200 ft. (60 m.) away from streams or lakes and use small amounts of biodegradable soap. Scatter strained dishwater.

4. LEAVE WHAT YOU FIND

It is easy to minimize site alterations by using a hammock. There is no need to remove rocks, twigs, or pine cones from a site. Avoid damaging live trees and plants.

- Preserve the past: observe, but do not touch, cultural or historic structures and artifacts.
- Leave rocks, plants and other natural objects as you find them.
- Avoid introducing or transporting non-native species.
- Do not build structures, furniture, or dig trenches.

5. MINIMIZE CAMPFIRE IMPACTS

Campfires are a fun, often integral part of camping for warmth and companionship. In some areas, you could conceivably hang your hammock near a fire, but this can be very dangerous. Where campfires are permitted, be wise and don't pitch a hammock too close to an open fire. Most camping hammocks and tarps are made with highly-flammable nylon fabrics.

◆ Campfires can cause lasting impacts to the backcountry. Use a lightweight stove for cooking and enjoy a candle lantern for light.
◆ Where fires are permitted, use established fire rings, fire pans, or mound fires.
◆ Keep fires small. Only use sticks from the ground that can be broken by hand.
◆ Burn all wood and coals to ash, put out campfires completely, then scatter cool ashes.

6. RESPECT WILDLIFE

In the Grand Canyon, park rangers permit hanging hammocks (responsibly) in campgrounds, but require that you remove hammocks during the day since elk and deer frequent the park and can get tangled in lines left suspended between trees. Ask your local campground for specific rules in your area.

Many hangers enjoy cooking or eating right out of a hammock, especially at breakfast. This can be an enjoyable and relaxing experience (hey! breakfast in bed!), but in areas or seasons where bears are problematic, like at certain shelters on the Appalachian Trail or at campgrounds where bears frequently visit, it is not recommended. The risk isn't worth the momentary pleasure. Spilled foods and wafting aromas that linger in the fabric and the camping area can be an issue. Eat and/or cook from a hammock only when lingering smells can be dispersed throughout the day (e.g., breakfast and lunch). Also, use only backpacking-style stoves where you can easily control the flame and protect yourself and your hammock gear.

- Observe wildlife from a distance. Do not follow or approach them.
- Never feed animals. Feeding wildlife damages their health, alters natural behaviors, and exposes them to predators and other dangers.
- Protect wildlife and your food by storing rations and trash securely. Always use a bear bag or canister.
- Control pets at all times, or leave them at home.
- Avoid wildlife during sensitive times: mating, nesting, raising young, or winter.

7. BE CONSIDERATE OF OTHER VISITORS

You can find hammock gear in a variety of colors including shark grey, bamboo yellow, sage green, and even various military camouflage patterns. While it is not required to blend in with nature, other visitors may appreciate not seeing a shocking pink tarp in the woods. To achieve this, be considerate of others by setting up your hammock out of view, regardless of the color of your gear. This is easily done if you follow Leave No Trace principles by staying at least 200 ft. (60 m.) away from trails, streams and lakes, and other shelters.

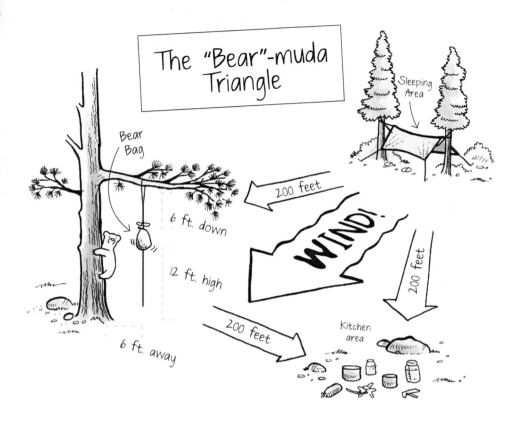

The "Bear"-muda Triangle

Bear Bag

Sleeping Area

200 feet

6 ft. down

WIND!

12 ft. high

200 feet

200 feet

Kitchen area

6 ft. away

Hammocks make lunch breaks and mid-hike rests a breeze. I always take a hammock with me on day hikes and look for great spots off trail where I can sit and relax. It's hardly a contest of comfort when the alternatives are rocks and fallen trees. The hammock makes a perfect lounger where I can loosen my sandals, prop up my feet, and watch other hikers as they pass my hidden relaxation station. With a hammock, I'm not restricted to the nearest stump along the trail for a break, so I can march away from the path where I won't bother anyone.

- ◆ Respect other visitors and protect the quality of their experience.
- ◆ Be courteous. Yield to other users on the trail.
- ◆ Step to the downhill side of the trail when encountering pack stock.
- ◆ Take breaks and camp away from trails and other visitors.
- ◆ Let nature's sounds prevail. Avoid loud voices and noises.

HANG IT UP!

With your preferred site safely selected following Leave No Trace guidelines, It's time to hang it up! You already know to look for trees between 12–15 ft. (4–4.5 m.) apart to create a fairly deep sag (for gathered-end hammocks), and to keep it chair height off the ground, right? But what about that magic 30° hang angle, and how high off the ground should you set the anchor point? It is fairly easy to achieve all these with a simple technique: **Three paces, reach, hang.** Here's how It's done.

1. THREE PACES—The average human step is around 30 in. (76 cm.). One pace (two steps) is about 60 in. (152 cm.). The optimal distance between support points is between 12 and 15 ft. (4 to 4.5 m.), so you need to find two trees that are about 3 paces (6 steps) apart. This distance provides space for both the hammock and the tarp (the tarp should extend past the ends of the hammock for maximum protection).

The further apart the trees, the higher the anchor points need to be in order to get a hang angle of 30 degrees. Anything further than 15 ft. (4.5 m.) and you won't be able to reach high enough on the tree to set the anchor points without climbing. When a hammock is hung too far apart and too high, the more the set-up will sag and the hammock won't lay as well.

With practice and experience, you'll be able to eyeball the perfect trees with confidence and consistency.

Start!

1 pace

2 paces

3 paces

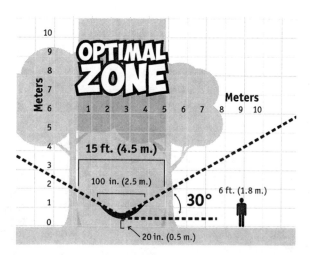
OPTIMAL ZONE

Meters

15 ft. (4.5 m.)

100 in. (2.5 m.)

30° 6 ft. (1.8 m.)

20 in. (0.5 m.)

The further apart the trees, the higher up you need to tie off your anchor points. Look for trees between 12–15 ft. (3.6–4.5 m.)—the "Optimal Zone."

Scan this QR code for an interactive hammock hang calculator.

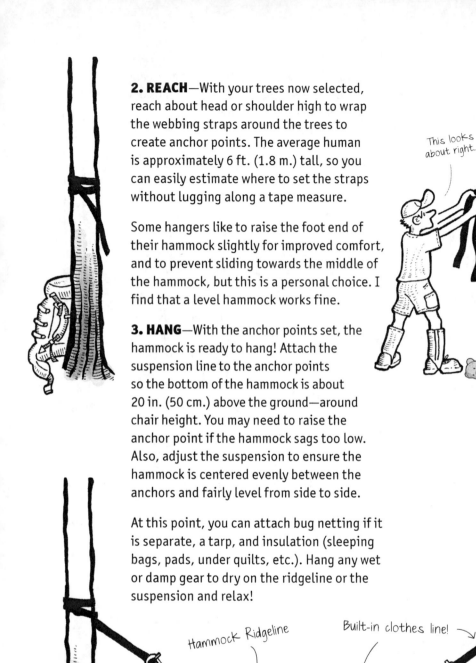

2. REACH—With your trees now selected, reach about head or shoulder high to wrap the webbing straps around the trees to create anchor points. The average human is approximately 6 ft. (1.8 m.) tall, so you can easily estimate where to set the straps without lugging along a tape measure.

This looks about right...

Some hangers like to raise the foot end of their hammock slightly for improved comfort, and to prevent sliding towards the middle of the hammock, but this is a personal choice. I find that a level hammock works fine.

3. HANG—With the anchor points set, the hammock is ready to hang! Attach the suspension line to the anchor points so the bottom of the hammock is about 20 in. (50 cm.) above the ground—around chair height. You may need to raise the anchor point if the hammock sags too low. Also, adjust the suspension to ensure the hammock is centered evenly between the anchors and fairly level from side to side.

At this point, you can attach bug netting if it is separate, a tarp, and insulation (sleeping bags, pads, under quilts, etc.). Hang any wet or damp gear to dry on the ridgeline or the suspension and relax!

Hammock Ridgeline

Built-in clothes line!

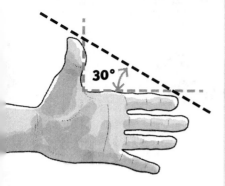

30°

★ **TIP:** One way to check your line for 30 degrees is by hand. Point your hand out straight with your thumb extended. Draw an imaginary line from the tip of your thumb to your index finger to approximate 30 degrees.

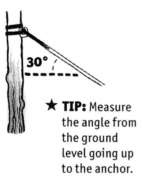

30°

★ **TIP:** Measure the angle from the ground level going up to the anchor.

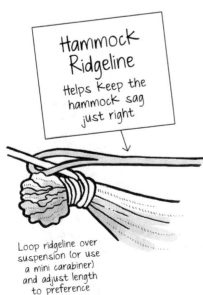

Hammock Ridgeline

Helps keep the hammock sag just right

Loop ridgeline over suspension (or use a mini carabiner) and adjust length to preference

BUT WHAT IF IT IS RAINING? Simply set the tarp first. You can follow the same steps to hang the tarp and then set up your hammock under a dry enclosure. Few tents provide the option to allow you to pitch the rain fly separately or before you pitch the main tent body. With a tarp, you can set up your hammock system and keep your gear protected.

See page 68 for more details on how to set up a hammock and tarp in the rain.

THE PERFECT SAG

The depth of the hammock's sag (with gathered-end hammocks) determines how flat you can lay. The sag can be adjusted for personal preferences. A simple, yet effective way to keep the same "sag" in your hammock each time you hang is to use a ridgeline that connects the two end points of the hammock. This ridgeline keeps the hammock from being pulled too tight.

Most hangers find a hammock ridgeline length of 100 in. (2.5 m.) about perfect. You can adjust the ridgeline to achieve the right "sag" for you.

A ridgeline is a great place to clip a light, hang a gear organizer, or dry out wet clothing. It comes in handy if you need bug netting over your hammock as it will keep the netting away from your body.

A ridgeline is not essential, but it is commonly used. It can get in the way when sitting in a hammock, so some hangers use a mini carabiner to quickly detach a ridgeline when not in use.

BREAKING IT DOWN
THE HAMMOCK

Gathered at the ends

I wonder if It's going to rain?

Simple!

Sleep on the diagonal for an ergonomic lay

Do a casual search for camping hammocks on the internet and you'll see dozens of brands available. Even the simple gathered-end hammocks have been enhanced and can get complex with added ridgelines, integrated no-see-um bug netting, or double-layered fabric. There are three basic styles of camping hammocks: **gathered-end, bridge, and spreader bar.**

GATHERED-END HAMMOCKS

Gathered-end hammocks are simple in construction and design—basically a rectangular piece of fabric gathered at the short ends. You can easily make your own gathered-end hammock by picking up a few yards of 1.9 oz. ripstop nylon fabric and whipping the ends, or sewing a channel on each end and tying it together with a line. **A standard size for many hammocks is 10 × 5 ft. (3 × 1.5 m.),** although you can find many smaller than that. Large hand-woven hammocks from South American can be larger still. Many manufacturers sew channels in the ends where a

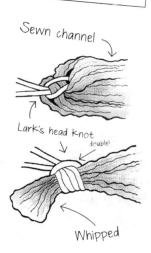

Gathered-End Hammocks

Sewn channel

Lark's head Knot
double!

Whipped

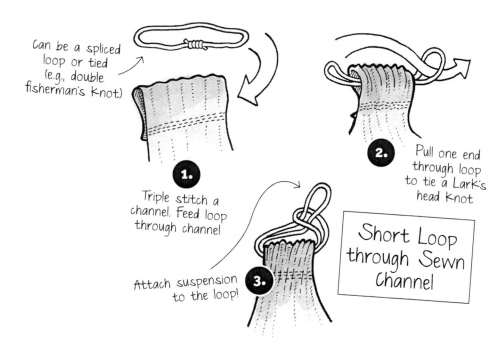

Can be a spliced loop or tied (e.g., double fisherman's Knot)

1. Triple stitch a channel. Feed loop through channel

2. Pull one end through loop to tie a Lark's head Knot

3. Attach suspension to the loop!

Short Loop through Sewn Channel

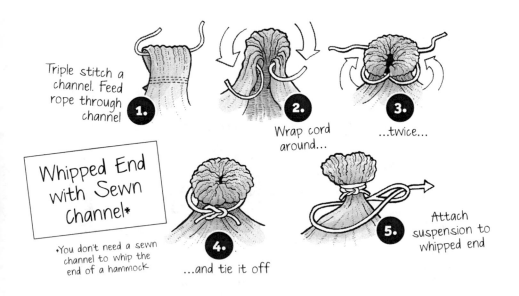

1. Triple stitch a channel. Feed rope through channel

2. Wrap cord around...

3. ...twice...

Whipped End with Sewn Channel*

*You don't need a sewn channel to whip the end of a hammock

4. ...and tie it off

5. Attach suspension to whipped end

cord or strap (e.g., Whoopie sling) can be threaded to gather the end and hang the hammock. Hennessy Hammock uses elaborate folding techniques to create custom pleats and sags in the hammock. While the techniques vary, the gathered-end hammock is essentially the same, and modeled after those found in South America.

Gathered-end hammocks are by far the most common camping and backpacking hammock because of their versatility, light weight, and simplicity—a tried-and-true workhorse hammock.

BRIDGE HAMMOCKS

Perhaps not as common, but one of the only hammock styles with a true head-to-foot "flat lay" is a bridge hammock. Jacks 'R' Better introduced the first commercially available bridge hammock in the *Bear Mountain Bridge Hammock*. This style is modeled after suspension bridges with catenary curved edges and uses two bars to help maintain its shape at the ends.

Those who have difficulty finding a good position using an gathered-end hammock may find a bridge style more to their liking. Bridge hammocks can also be made, but the template is more complicated. You can find instructions on HammockForums.net.

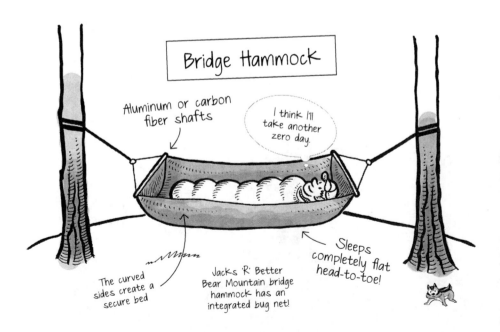

Bridge Hammock

Aluminum or carbon fiber shafts

I think I'll take another zero day.

The curved sides create a secure bed

Jacks 'R' Better Bear Mountain bridge hammock has an integrated bug net!

Sleeps completely flat head-to-toe!

SPREADER BAR HAMMOCKS

A common backyard lounging hammock is the spreader bar hammock. The spreader bars attempt to make the hammock as flat as possible, unlike the bridge design. These hammocks are designed for temporary lounging and are not useful for overnight camping. There are, however, a few camping hammocks that use a spreader bar design like the Crazy Creek *LEX* and the Lawson Hammock *Blue Ridge*, which incorporate a bug net, tent poles, and tarp for complete protection.

★ **TIP:** Keep a spreader bar hammock from tipping by guying out the corners or the sides.

The spreader bar design is prone to tipping because the center of gravity is so high.

HYBRID DESIGNS

Hybrid designs combine different elements such as spreader bars, rope-tied ends, and computer-modeled designs. Some noteworthy examples include a genuine two-person hammock like the *Vertex* by Clark Jungle Hammock, where each occupant sleeps in his/her own "nest." There are even single-point designs like the *Bat Hammock* by Mosquito Hammock that is perfectly suited for multi-day rock climbing activities where you can hang right off the cliff face.

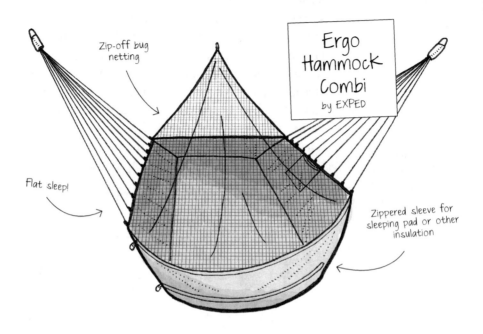

Zip-off bug netting

Ergo Hammock Combi
by EXPED

Flat sleep!

Zippered sleeve for sleeping pad or other insulation

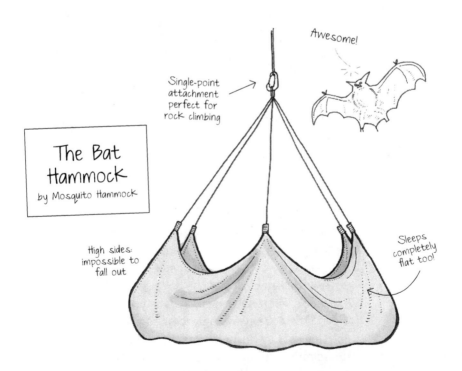

Single-point attachment perfect for rock climbing

Awesome!

The Bat Hammock
by Mosquito Hammock

High sides: impossible to fall out

Sleeps completely flat too!

Hammocks are great for tinkering and experimenting, so many people who start with one style often try others—building and testing as they create their perfect system. Many avid hangers have experimented with new insulation methods and materials that have improved the way people stay warm. Other discoveries and inventions have revolutionized hammock tarps, suspension lines, and even packing methods.

TWO PEOPLE IN ONE HAMMOCK?

Many people, especially those transitioning from tents, wonder if more than one person can sleep comfortably in a single hammock. The short answer is a definite "maybe." Yes, large hammocks can fit more people, but no, it isn't very comfortable for sleeping. Most hammocks, regardless of size, are designed for a single occupant. For some, the desire to double is to remain close, while others want to share gear, maybe saving some pack weight in the process.

Think of a hammock more like an upgraded individual sleeping pad. In tents, most people use their own pads and sleeping bags, but sleep close together. You can still achieve cozy proximity in hammocks with good site selection by hanging hammocks side-by-side or stacking them. I often do this when I camp with my family, as it is helpful to have my kids within reach. Occasionally I've brought one (or two) of my kids into my hammock with me when they couldn't sleep, but I was uncomfortable and cold.

A hammock naturally wraps and conforms to your body, one of the reasons they are so comfortable. Adding more people creates awkward ridges and minimizes the comfort for those inside. To work well, occupants must move and turn together, like synchronized swimmers. Personally, I prefer having separate hammocks within close proximity. I think this is the best of both words: individualized comfort, but chummy closeness.

I'm freezing and cramped in here!!

While it is difficult to share a single sleeping bag and under quilt between two hammocks, other gear can be easily shared like a tarp, a gear loft, and a floor mat. There really isn't a lot of weight difference between a large double sleeping bag and two individual bags. If you want to go lightweight, I recommend investing in down-filled top quilts. These quilts save weight by removing the back panel and eliminate unneeded features like zippers and draft tubes.

HAMMOCK (AND TARP) REPAIRS

The most common repair on hammocks and tarps are for small holes and tears. These are usually avoided by setting up a hammock and a rain fly/tarp without having them touch the ground (the usual hole-poking suspect). Once, while setting up a new hammock, a gust of wind caught it like a kite and swept it to the ground where it promptly ripped a hole. With nylon and polyester camping hammocks, the best solution for small repairs is to use TEAR-AID®, Type A. TEAR-AID is a flexible, airtight, watertight, puncture-resistant, industrial-strength patch that protects against abrasion, moisture, saltwater, UV sunlight, and extreme temperatures. It's unique composition stretches and recovers its original shape. Just peel and stick a patch to apply. The hole on my hammock was right near the bottom—a high stress area—but the patch has held firm through many hangs.

You can use TEAR-AID for both hammocks and tarps made from synthetic fabric. Hammocks with large holes and/or tears should be retired (or recycled into other do-it-yourself gear, like stuff sacks) because the risk of the fabric failing is high. Sewing patches in hammocks will only further weaken the fabric and is not recommended.

Prevention is your best defense against hammock rips and tears. In practice, this is fairly easy as you can set up your entire shelter without it touching the ground or nearby objects. Don't sleep with sharp objects in your pockets or wear clothing in the hammock that may pose a puncture problem. Carefully repack your gear once you are done. Don't set up your hammock too close to branches, twigs, or thorns.

BREAKING IT DOWN
SUSPENSION & ANCHOR POINTS

Who needs trees?

Thick webbing straps are universally accepted as the *de-facto* standard for creating anchor points, especially around trees. But when it comes to suspension lines and hardware, variation is the name of the game: Whoopie slings, tri-glides, Dutch clips, descender rings—perhaps the most variation in hammock camping comes in connecting your hammock to the anchor point. By the time this book is published, I have no doubt that someone will invent a new way to attach a hammock to an anchor point. Why so many choices? Why not just a rope and a few good knots? The reasons are varied, and usually boil down to what is fast, light, and easy. Your own style will determine which method(s) works best for you. Perhaps you'll have a few you'll try, just for fun! I know I do.

ANCHOR POINTS

Typically, the first step in hanging a hammock is to set the anchor points. Using the method described under "How To Hang" can help determine how high and far apart to set the anchor points.

Tying rope directly around a tree can be potentially harmful to the cambium layer. The best way to protect tree bark is to use non-stretching polyester or polypropylene webbing (anything from 1 in. (2.5 cm.) to 2 in. (5 cm.) wide) commonly called "tree straps" or "tree huggers" to wrap around the tree. Avoid nylon straps as they stretch too much.

The webbing helps distribute the weight around the tree and leaves little or no evidence once you remove your hammock.

The length of the tree straps is variable and should depend on the size of the trees you expect to encounter out in the backcountry. A common length is 6 ft. (1.8 m.), but can be as short as 3 ft. (91 cm.) or as long as 10 ft. (3 m.) or more. Many hangers use the webbing not only as the tree hugger and anchor point, but also as the suspension line, so the strap must be long enough to accommodate the tree diameter and the distance to hammock.

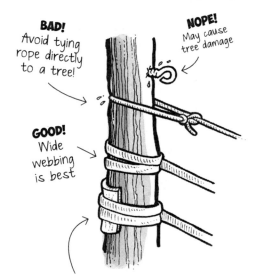

BAD!
Avoid tying rope directly to a tree!

NOPE!
May cause tree damage

GOOD!
Wide webbing is best

BETTER!
Use a small square of closed-cell foam padding for extended hangs in one place

Most webbing straps have eye loops sewn or tied into each end. A figure-8-on-a-bight is a secure knot if you're making your own webbing strap and don't want to sew. Once set with weight, a figure-8 will be difficult to untie so consider it permanent. With these eye loops, you can clip a carabiner, Dutch clip, or other connector to easily attach the webbing around the tree.

There are several methods for wrapping webbing around a tree. This method works well: wrap one time around a tree, and then connect the two eye loops with a carabiner. If you have a carabiner or Dutch clip attached into one eye loop, you can quickly clip or slip the standing end of the webbing to the clip for a complete connection. Without hardware, you can also slip the standing end of the webbing through an eye loop. Carabiners and Dutch clips are quick and allow easy repositioning if you need to make adjustments. Feeding the webbing through the loop requires no extra hardware and is therefore

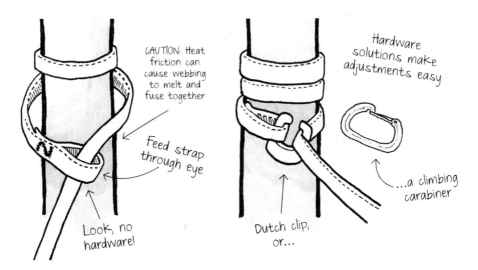

CAUTION: Heat friction can cause webbing to melt and fuse together

Feed strap through eye

Look, no hardware!

Hardware solutions make adjustments easy

...a climbing carabiner

Dutch clip, or...

slightly lighter, but it takes a little more time to assemble and disassemble. Intricate lashings or extra wraps around a tree make it difficult to adjust a hammock, and also take longer to disassemble.

With the tree straps attached, you now have an anchor point where you can attach your hammock's suspension lines, or you can use your long straps as suspension lines if they can reach your hammock.

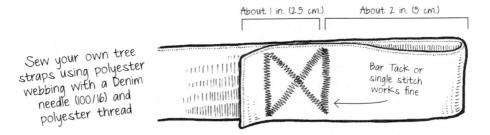

About 1 in. (2.5 cm.)

About 2 in. (5 cm.)

Sew your own tree straps using polyester webbing with a Denim needle (100/16) and polyester thread

Bar Tack or single stitch works fine

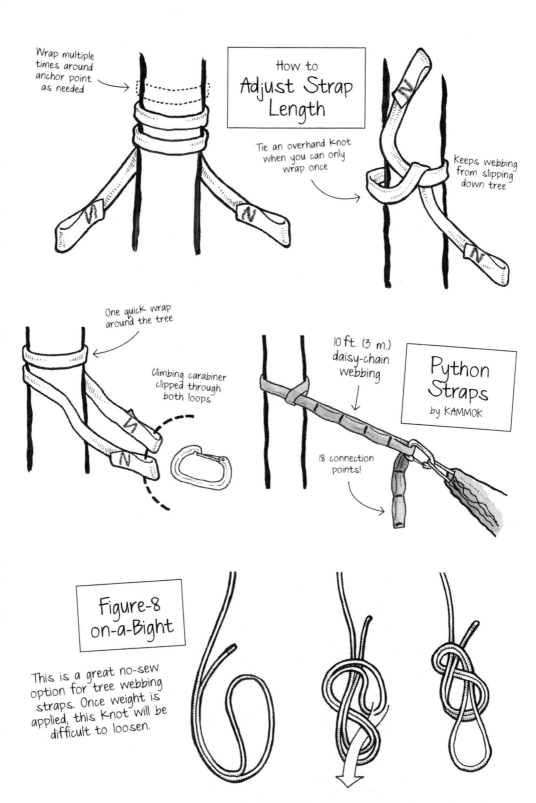

Wrap multiple times around anchor point as needed

How to **Adjust Strap Length**

Tie an overhand knot when you can only wrap once

Keeps webbing from slipping down tree

One quick wrap around the tree

Climbing carabiner clipped through both loops

10 ft. (3 m.) daisy-chain webbing

Python Straps by KAMMOK

18 connection points!

Figure-8 on-a-Bight

This is a great no-sew option for tree webbing straps. Once weight is applied, this knot will be difficult to loosen.

SUSPENSION LINE

WHOOPIE SLINGS—One interesting innovation in the past few years is the Whoopie sling. These adjustable loops have been used for many years by arborists for tree pruning or other dendrology. Using hollow core rope, a loop (the sling) is created by feeding the line through the core creating a spliced choker. Like a Chinese finger trap, the tension is applied from both sides and the outer rope constricts the splice, locking the size of the loop. Whoopie slings are designed with two eye loops: a spliced, fixed loop on one end, which is attached to the hammock (typically with a Lark's head knot), and an adjustable loop, which is attached to the webbing anchor. Some Whoopie slings are made with a small bead on the adjustable eye loop to keep from pulling the loop into the splice.

Whoopie slings are more often made with Dyneema cord—strong, yet lightweight synthetic rope (commonly called Amsteel Blue) that is manufactured in a variety of colors. Amsteel has the distinction of being as strong as steel for its size and very lightweight. It does not rebound and also floats on water. Whoopie slings are often made with 7/64 in. Amsteel (rated to 1,600 lbs.), or even 1/8 in. Amsteel (rated to 2,500 lbs.). Whoopie slings are easily adjustable.

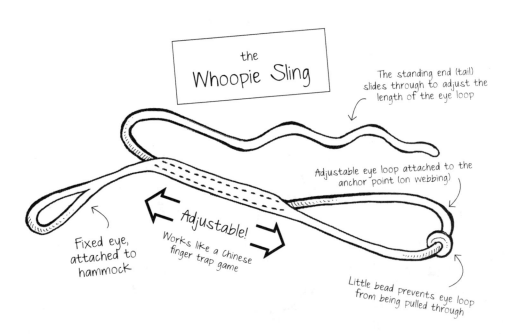

the
Whoopie Sling

The standing end (tail) slides through to adjust the length of the eye loop

Adjustable eye loop attached to the anchor point (on webbing)

Fixed eye, attached to hammock

Adjustable!
Works like a Chinese finger trap game

Little bead prevents eye loop from being pulled through

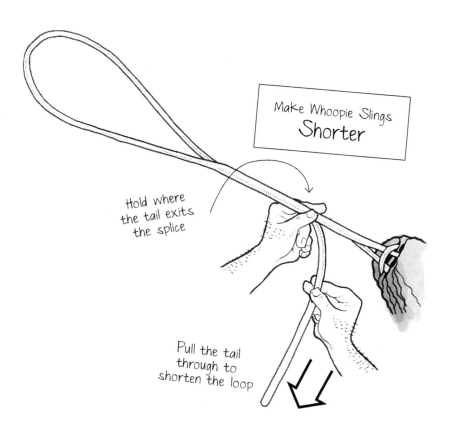

Make Whoopie Slings
Shorter

Hold where
the tail exits
the splice

Pull the tail
through to
shorten the loop

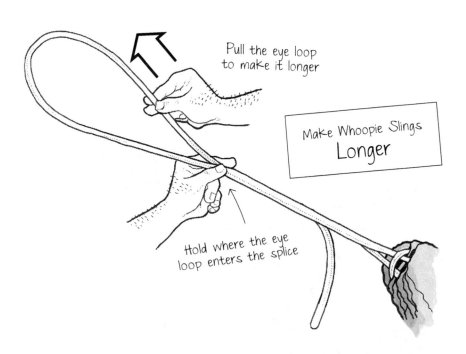

Pull the eye loop
to make it longer

Make Whoopie Slings
Longer

Hold where the eye
loop enters the splice

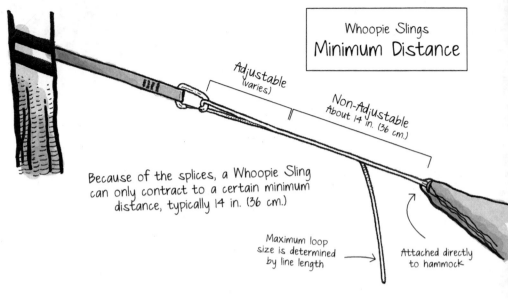

Adjustable
(varies)

Non-Adjustable
About 14 in. (36 cm.)

Because of the splices, a Whoopie Sling can only contract to a certain minimum distance, typically 14 in. (36 cm.)

Maximum loop size is determined by line length

Attached directly to hammock

When Whoopie Slings Are Too Long

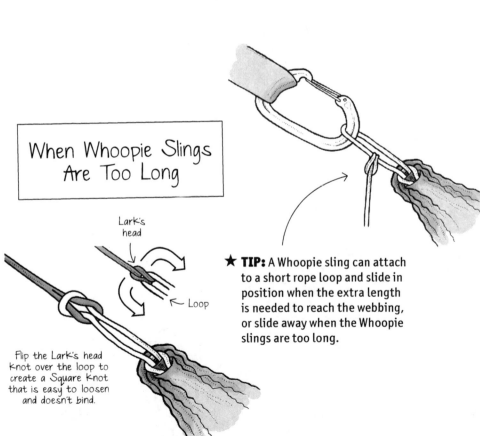

Lark's head

Loop

★ **TIP:** A Whoopie sling can attach to a short rope loop and slide in position when the extra length is needed to reach the webbing, or slide away when the Whoopie slings are too long.

Flip the Lark's head knot over the loop to create a Square Knot that is easy to loosen and doesn't bind.

★ **TIP:** Going ultralight? Webbing straps can double as compression straps on a backpack or to tie-down bulky gear like bear canisters or sleeping pads. I've even used one as a belt.

WEBBING—As cool and hip as Whoopie slings are, webbing straps are equally easy to use in adjusting and pitching hammocks. Since you're already using webbing straps to create an anchor point to a tree, all you need are straps long enough to reach your hammock. The long, standing end of the webbing becomes the adjustable part of the suspension. By using hardware options like cinch buckles or tri-glides, you can quickly adjust and secure your hammock.

ROPE—Most commercial hammocks come with rope already attached to the hammock, including the Hennessy, ENO, Trek Light Gear, Grand Trunk, KAMMOK, Planet Hammock, and many others. Hennessy models come with a long length of rope for its suspension line. More commonly, the rope is just a short loop attached via a Lark's head knot at the end of the hammock. This provides a great attachment point for a Whoopie sling, a climbing carabiner, toggle, Elephant Trunks, or descender rings.

Rope is easier to tie than webbing. However, knots will degrade the rating of the rope, can be difficult to untie once set, and are not as easy to adjust. Always use high-quality climbing rope with a hammock.

Marlinespike hitch or sewn loop

Toggle

Rope

Climbing carabiner

Weave webbing strap through descender rings

Rope

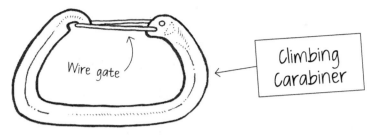

Wire gate

Climbing Carabiner

(Enlarged to show detail)

the Mini-biner

Great for tarps, under quilts, and small clips, but not strong enough for hammocks

HARDWARE CONNECTORS

There are a variety of connectors to attach your preferred suspension system to the webbing. Here are a few of the most common methods:

CARABINERS—Used in climbing and rappelling, these metal clips are great for connecting hammocks to suspension and webbing, but make sure the 'biners are rated for climbing. Key-chain and mini carabiners will quickly bend and fail when too much weight is applied and should be avoided. Quick-release wire gate carabiners are some of the easiest to use, as you don't need the locking features some carabiners have.

CINCH BUCKLES—These buckles look similar to tri-glides, but the center post can move. The cinch buckle is also used to adjust long webbing straps that run from the tree to the hammock. Tie a half hitch after the buckle to prevent slipping.

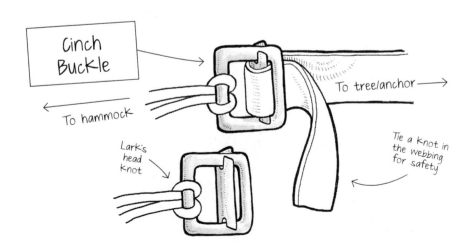

Cinch Buckle

← To hammock

To tree/anchor →

Lark's head knot

Tie a knot in the webbing for safety

DESCENDER RINGS—These small metal rings are also borrowed from the climbing and rappelling community. Originally used to facilitate the recovery of rope on a rappel, you can use two descender rings together to adjust the length of long webbing between tree and hammock. Weave the webbing strap through both rings and then back through the top one. Descender rings require a safety knot (half hitch) to prevent the webbing from slipping.

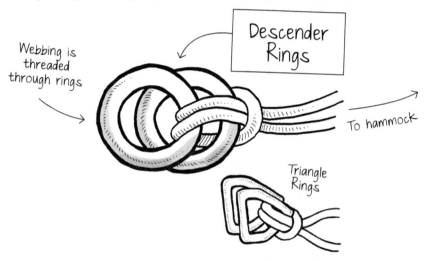

Webbing is threaded through rings

Descender Rings

To hammock

Triangle Rings

DUTCH CLIPS—This clip was developed by "Dutch" of DutchWare and resembles a horse shoe. These clips are very lightweight and have no moving parts, making set-up easy and hassle-free. Dutch clips work in place of climbing carabiners to easily connect a webbing strap around a tree or other support.

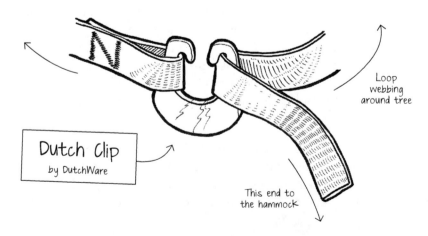

Loop webbing around tree

Dutch Clip
by DutchWare

This end to the hammock

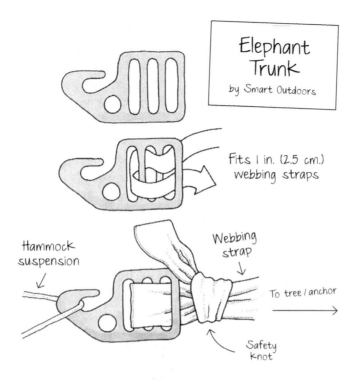

Elephant
Trunk
by Smart Outdoors

Fits 1 in. (2.5 cm.)
webbing straps

Hammock
suspension

Webbing
strap

To tree / anchor

Safety
knot

ELEPHANT TRUNKS—Another product for creating an anchor point is the *Elephant Trunk* from Smart Outdoors. These aluminum-cast hardware devices combine tri-glides with a hook so you can attach webbing straps to one end and the hammock suspension line (e.g., Whoopie slings) to the hook.

KNOTS & LASHINGS—Before all the innovative clips, glides, buckles, toggles, and slings were used, the most common way to secure a hammock to webbing was through knots and lashings. This is lighter than using extra hardware and there is less to misplace. Hennessy introduced the "figure-8" lashing that ties directly to the webbing, creating a secure anchor point. Other knots or lashings can be used, but some ropes hold better than others. Climbing and accessory ropes work better with knots than slippery Dyneema (the material used to make Whoopie slings).

One disadvantage to knots and lashings is they are not as easy to adjust as Whoopie slings or hardware options with webbing straps. Some secure knots are used in climbing and rappelling, including the figure-8 knot and bowline. However, these knots will bind once

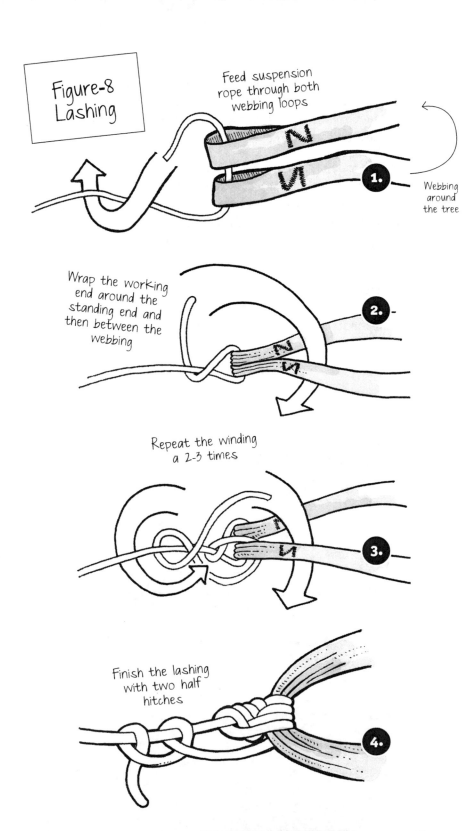

Figure-8 Lashing

Feed suspension rope through both webbing loops

1. Webbing around the tree

Wrap the working end around the standing end and then between the webbing

2.

Repeat the winding a 2-3 times

3.

Finish the lashing with two half hitches

4.

weight is applied, so they are not practical if you are planning to untie and adjust the rope. Webbing on webbing, or rope on webbing can heat up and melt once pressure is applied. Check for wear and damage after each hang.

One knot that works well is a slippery Lark's head or girth hitch tied to a climbing carabiner at the anchor point. I first tried this method on my Hennessy Hammock, using the stock rope that came with the kit. I got tired of lashing the rope because I always had to make some minor adjustment to the hammock before I was satisfied.

The slippery Lark's head worked so well that I used it on other camping hammocks. I used 5 mm. climbing rope, which held firm, even in heavy downpours. What I love about the slippery Lark's head is with a quick pull on the standing end, I can release the knot to adjust or pack up.

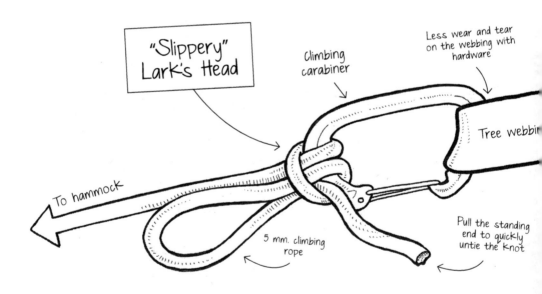

"Slippery" Lark's Head

Climbing carabiner

Less wear and tear on the webbing with hardware

Tree webbing

To hammock

5 mm. climbing rope

Pull the standing end to quickly untie the knot

★ **TIP:** Always test your hang a few times in the safety of your backyard before going into the backcountry.

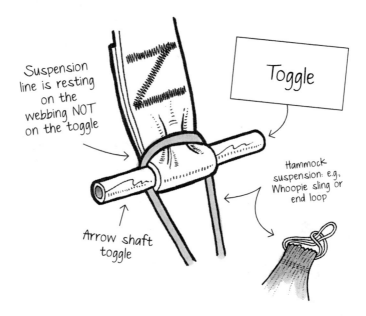

Suspension line is resting on the webbing NOT on the toggle

Toggle

Hammock suspension: e.g., Whoopie sling or end loop

Arrow shaft toggle

TOGGLES—A toggle can be almost anything: an aluminum stake, a mini carabiner, a pencil, a small stick, etc. To use, place the toggle into a loop in some webbing (either a fixed eye on the webbing or an adjustable loop like the Marlinespike hitch) and place the suspension line around the webbing. The toggle does not directly bear any weight, so it does not need to be very strong. However, make sure the suspension line (e.g., Whoopie sling) is looped over the webbing and not on the toggle or it may fail.

This is my most used and preferred method for connecting my suspension strap (Whoopie slings) to my webbing. Toggles are simple and easy to replace if they get lost on the trail. You can also buy premade toggles from several manufacturers.

★ **TIP:** Carbon fiber and aluminum arrowhead shafts make excellent lightweight toggles. Other toggle options include titanium or aluminum stakes (cut in half) and metal connector sections from old fiberglass tent poles. **Don't lose your toggle**—carefully drill a small hole in one end where you can attach a string to keep the toggle permanently attached to the webbing.

TRI-GLIDES—This metal buckle is commonly used with camping hammocks. The metal tri-glide is a single piece of metal with two long holes where the webbing is threaded. Slide the webbing through the tri-glide to adjust the length of the strap. Tie a safety knot (half hitch) to prevent the webbing from slipping.

Metal Tri-glide

To hammock

MARLINESPIKE HITCH—This non-binding, temporary knot is tied anywhere along the length of the webbing to create a place where a toggle can be positioned. This hitch is fairly easy to tie and has the benefit of coming apart easily once you remove the toggle.

Be sure to place your suspension line on the knot and not directly on the toggle. A lightweight toggle works because it doesn't bear the full force of the load.

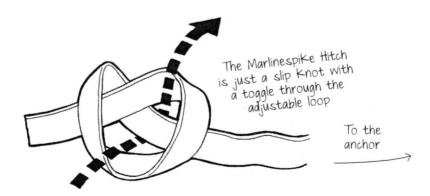

The Marlinespike Hitch is just a slip knot with a toggle through the adjustable loop

To the anchor

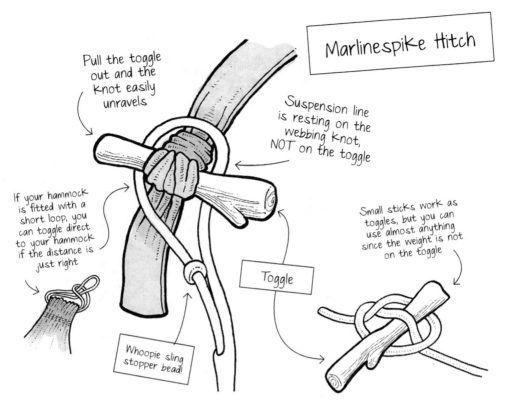

Pull the toggle out and the knot easily unravels

Suspension line is resting on the webbing knot, NOT on the toggle

If your hammock is fitted with a short loop, you can toggle direct to your hammock if the distance is just right

Small sticks work as toggles, but you can use almost anything since the weight is not on the toggle

Toggle

Whoopie sling stopper bead!

The marlinespike hitch is essentially a slip knot with the toggle placed in the noose. Tie this "slippery" overhand knot by pulling a loop through the hole. The toggle is slipped through the loop and then the knot is dressed up and tightened. Place the hammock suspension line over the dressed knot and you're ready to hang!

This hitch is a common connector because it is easy to tie, requires no extra hardware, and makes it easy to adjust the length of the webbing or anchor point.

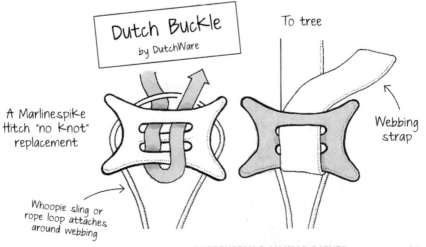

Dutch Buckle
by DutchWare

To tree

A Marlinespike Hitch "no knot" replacement

Webbing strap

Whoopie sling or rope loop attaches around webbing

BREAKING IT DOWN
STAYING DRY

Tarp angled to deflect rain

I love it when it rains!

Hiking pole used to create a "porch"

Staying above the puddles!

When it comes to weather protection, some like full coverage while others prefer to go topless. There's no right or wrong answer here, and your choice depends on many factors: weight, cost, bulk, coverage, versatility, ease-of-use, and personalization, to name a few.

In moderate conditions, almost any tarp can be modified for good coverage, ventilation, and privacy. Larger tarps offer more protection and options.

In practice, the art of staying dry in a hammock is pretty simple. With a good tarp, some drip lines, and a weather cover, you can stay protected from all angles and have complete privacy.

Really small!

the
Dutch
Hook

Carabiner replacement for tarps by DutchWare

PITCH-PERFECT TARPS

TARP RIDGELINES

★ **TIP:** Add a drip line to your tarp ridgeline if it runs under the tarp. See **page 79**.

Set up the tarp before the hammock to keep you and your gear dry in adverse conditions such as heavy rain, snow, and wind. You can use knots or any number of hardware options to tie up a tarp. The amount of versatility means you can pick what works best for you to balance weight, strength, ease-of-use, and personal taste.

Most tarp ridgelines fall under one of two types: end-only or full-length. End-only lines essentially eliminate the rope between the tarp tie-outs, which can reduce some weight. Full-length ridgelines run the entire length of the tarp and can be strung under or over the tarp. Both styles can be installed and packed with the tarp to make set up easier.

With a full-length ridgeline, you can set the line first and then adjust the tarp along the line to center it. It is often easier to center a tarp between the supports with a full-length ridgeline than with end-only lines.

the
S-Biner
by Nite Ize

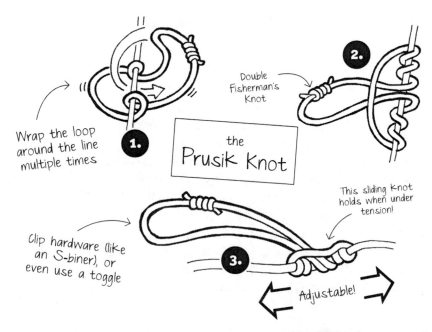

Wrap the loop around the line multiple times

Double Fisherman's Knot

1.

the
Prusik Knot

2.

Clip hardware (like an S-biner), or even use a toggle

This sliding knot holds when under tension!

3.

Adjustable!

Hanging the tarp over a full-length ridgeline provides additional structure and can be preferred during extreme conditions, such as a wet snow storm or when strong winds put additional pressure on the tarp. In this way the ridgeline can help support extra weight. With the ridgeline running under the tarp, it also provides convenient points for hanging gear to air dry, clipping on a light, or attaching a bug net.

CREATING THE "V"

Whether you use a full-length ridgeline or tie-outs on the ends, a great method for attaching the tarp ridgeline to the tree support is to create a "V" shape. For end-only tie-outs, tie one end of the line to the tarp using two half-hitches, then wrap the standing end around the tree and tie it back to the tarp using an adjustable taut-line hitch. For a full-length ridgeline, tie one end to a mini-biner or an S-biner then clip the biner to the tarp. The running end wraps around the tree, clips through the 'biner, and then runs either over or under the tarp through a second carabiner on the opposite side. Make another "V" around the second tree and then secure to the carabiner.

With the "V" space created, the hammock suspension can swing back and forth between the "V" with little or no collision against the tarp ridgeline.

To tarp

the
KnotBone
by Nite Ize

Loop around tree

!

DON'T LIKE TYING KNOTS? There are multiple ways you can secure a tarp ridgeline without tying a single knot (although knots are handy). Most no-knot methods require some kind of hardware alternative like a Figure-9 from Nite Ize or a mini carabiner. There have been many devices developed in the hammock community for tying off a tarp ridgeline, a few include the Tarp Flyz, the Tarp Key, and the Tarp Cross. Each of these hardware options are very lightweight yet strong enough to bear the pull of the tarp. No-knot hardware usually requires you to wrap the line a few times around the hardware for a secure hold.

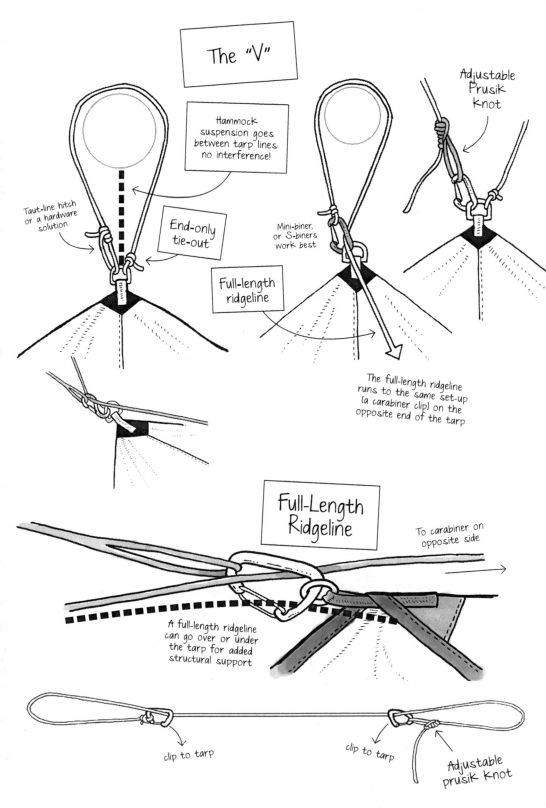

The "V"

Hammock suspension goes between tarp lines: no interference!

Taut-line hitch or a hardware solution

End-only tie-out

Mini-biner, or S-biners work best

Full-length ridgeline

Adjustable Prusik Knot

The full-length ridgeline runs to the same set-up (a carabiner clip) on the opposite end of the tarp

Full-Length Ridgeline

To carabiner on opposite side

A full-length ridgeline can go over or under the tarp for added structural support

clip to tarp

clip to tarp

Adjustable prusik knot

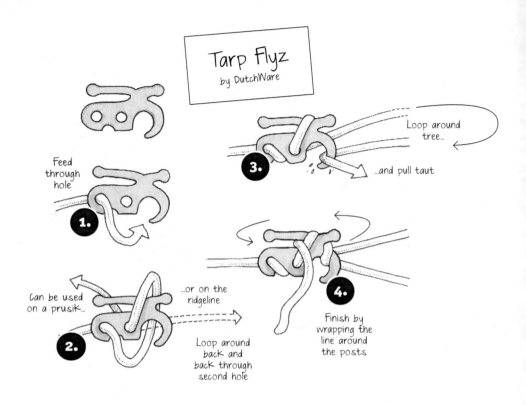

Tarp Flyz
by DutchWare

Feed through hole

1.

2. Can be used on a prusik...

...or on the ridgeline

Loop around back and back through second hole

3. Loop around tree...

...and pull taut

4. Finish by wrapping the line around the posts

the Figure-9
by Nite Ize

Push loop through hole and around key

Pull taut and lock the rope in the slot

Attach the hardware to the ridgeline directly or to a prusik for adjustability.

Loop around tree

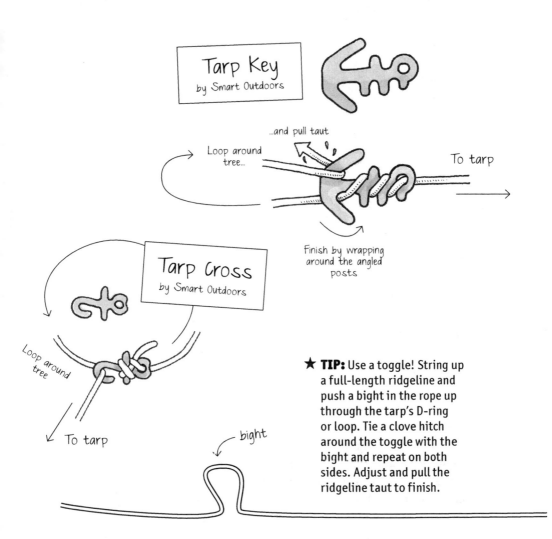

Tarp Key
by Smart Outdoors

Loop around tree...

...and pull taut

To tarp

Finish by wrapping around the angled posts

Tarp Cross
by Smart Outdoors

Loop around tree

To tarp

bight

★ **TIP:** Use a toggle! String up a full-length ridgeline and push a bight in the rope up through the tarp's D-ring or loop. Tie a clove hitch around the toggle with the bight and repeat on both sides. Adjust and pull the ridgeline taut to finish.

PROTECTION FROM ABOVE

To better fit the shape and unique attributes of a hammock, a few specialized tarp styles have grown in popularity, including asymmetric (a-sym), diamond, hexagonal, and fully-enclosed "winter" tarps. Some manufacturers have created unique design combinations including asymmetric hexagonal tarps, but these styles are not as common. Most camping and backpacking tarps use lightweight, waterproof polyester and nylon fabrics that can pack down small. Silicone-impregnated nylon (or silnylon), is a popular lightweight fabric choice, but ultralight backpackers prefer cuben fiber and spinnaker fabrics, which weigh half as much as silnylon but can cost twice as much. Each tarp style and fabric choice has its own pros and cons for weight, durability, bulk, and cost (not to mention style and individual vender craftsmanship).

Inexpensive "industrial" tarps can be found in retail shops and work fine for hammock camping, but they may be too heavy and bulky for backpacking.

ASYMMETRIC AND FAIR-WEATHER TARPS

Standard with most Hennessy Hammocks is the asymmetric (a-sym) tarp. These tarps are sewn in a parallelogram shape to mirror how a person lays in the hammock. Large ponchos can even be used as an asymmetric tarp (Hennessy actually sells an a-sym tarp that zips up as a hoodless poncho). An a-sym tarp is sufficient in moderate rain storms, but keep in mind that smaller tarps require greater skill to keep the hammock and gear dry in adverse conditions. With an a-sym tarp, for example, sleeping in a diagonal position in the opposite direction of the tarp fabric may expose your head and feet to the elements.

DIAMOND TARPS

A square tarp, pitched corner-to-corner as a diamond, provides fair to great coverage of a hammock, depending on its size. A basic 8 × 8 ft. (2.4 × 2.4 m.) tarp creates a ridgeline of more than 11 ft. (3.3 m.)— plenty of room to cover most hammocks. Diamond tarps work great except in sideways downpours, similar to a-sym tarps. An advantage of a diamond tarp, like the a-sym, is it requires only two guy points so it is quick to pitch.

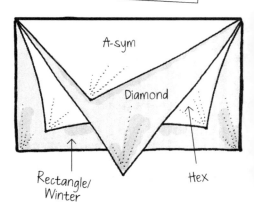

Tarp Coverage Comparison

A-sym

Diamond

Rectangle/ Winter

Hex

★ **TIP:** During a heavy downpour you might feel "mist" coming from the inside of your tarp. This could simply be condensation droplets jarring loose. In rare cases with silnylon tarps if you have pitched the tarp TOO TIGHT the pressure (PSI) from the rain may push micro-droplets through the fabric. To stop this, pitch the tarp slightly LOOSE so the fabric can flex, reducing the pressure.

Common Hammock Camping Tarp Styles

	SIDE VIEW	TOP VIEW	ISOMETRIC VIEW

+ Light!
+ Easier to pitch
- Minimal Coverage
- Less privacy

+ Full Coverage
+ More Pitching Options
+ Privacy
+ Versatile
- Heavy
- More complex to pitch

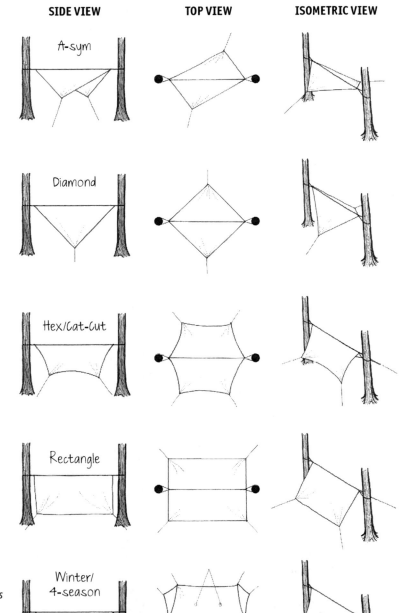

A-sym

Diamond

Hex/Cat-Cut

Rectangle

Winter/
4-season

HEX TARPS

Hexagon-shaped (hex) tarps are common for hammock camping. Hex tarps typically have catenary cut edges that create a taut pitch and virtually eliminate material flapping in the wind. If a hex tarp has enough side tie-outs, you can fold in the ends to create make-shift doors, completely sealing you off in all directions. Hex tarps have "beaks" that provide additional coverage over the ridgeline.

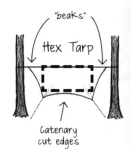

"beaks"

Hex Tarp

Catenary cut edges

FOUR-SEASON WINTER TARPS

Full-coverage tarps, or "winter" tarps are best for four-season camping when you need maximum protection from the elements. Some describe the winter tarp as a four-sided wall tent, and in some cases this is accurate. Winter tarps usually have extra fabric on the sides that can be turned and pitched to seal off the open ends on regular and hexagonal tarps. Some manufacturers sell after-market "doors" as an optional addition to hexagonal or rectangular tarps.

Winter tarps are often much wider than any other tarp style so the sides can be pitched low, eliminating drafts and ground splashes. These tarps usually feature side panel guy points to create a roomy interior and to strengthen the tarp in strong wind gusts.

Large tarps also provide good privacy for changing clothes, etc., but they can be more complicated to pitch, can weigh more, and can require extra hardware (e.g., stakes, guylines).

Winter Tarp
with doors closed

End flaps or "doors" can be closed for maximum protection or opened for more ventilation

Side pull-o... increase ro... inside tarp strengthen tarp in the ...

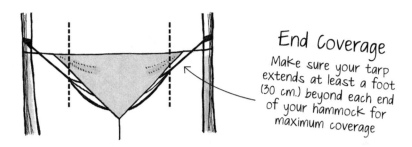

End Coverage

Make sure your tarp extends at least a foot (30 cm.) beyond each end of your hammock for maximum coverage

PROTECTION FROM BELOW

In highly-impacted areas, such as near popular campgrounds, you might find compacted soil that collects water and sends splashes underneath your hammock. A first good defense against ground splashes goes back to site selection. For example, a spot over thick moss or layers of pine needles will absorb more water. Additional protection can be handled with large tarps that pitch all the way to the ground, weather under covers, or fully-enclosed hammock socks.

WEATHER UNDER COVERS

A weather cover or "shield" is like a second hammock made of waterproof fabric that hangs below the hammock and insulation. An under cover can double as a gear sling when not used to protect from ground splashes. Under covers are great in wet conditions.

HAMMOCK SOCKS

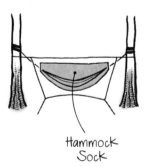

Hammock Sock

A weather cover that encloses the entire hammock is called a "hammock sock." Imagine a tube of fabric cinched at each end and you'll have a good visual. Hammock socks are great protection from ground splashes and also add warmth by blocking wind drafts and creating dead air space. Some hangers have used hammock socks without tarps, creating a floating bivvy. Be careful: depending on conditions, condensation can collect on the fabric unless moist exhaled air can escape. Like ground bivvy sacks, hammock socks can be constructed with both breathable and non-breathable/waterproof fabrics to provide the best combination of breathability and water protection.

PRIVACY

Some people are concerned that hammocks don't provide full coverage like a tent when privacy is desired. This can be an issue with a small a-sym or diamond tarp, but large "hex" or rectangular tarps provide ample coverage, especially when pitched low or as a screen. Winter tarps or those with add-on doors provide complete privacy, just like a tent.

I prefer to change behind or under a tarp where I have more room, rather than writhing in a tent. With a tarp, I can stand or sit comfortably and dress with less frustration.

Good site selection and proper set-up are two factors in getting the most privacy from tarps.

★ **TIP:** Place your change of clothes in your hammock for easy reach. Carry a small 3 × 3 ft. (1 × 1 m.) piece of Tyvek® wrap or plastic sheet as a ground cloth/foot mat to keep your feet and gear off the ground when you're changing clothes.

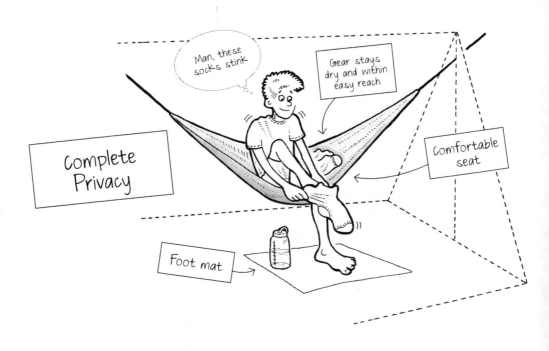

THE LOOSE ENDS

STOPPING THE DRIP

In major downpours, rain water can run down the suspension lines and soak the hammock from the ends. You can redirect this water by attaching a drip line along the suspension line. Water will flow to the lowest point, so once it hits the drip line it will flow down the line to the ground. Besides drip lines, some hardware options can re-route the water, include descender rings and cinch buckles, etc. The hardware does the work of a drip line automatically. If positioned correctly under the tarp, even the running end of a Whoopie Sling can work as a drip line.

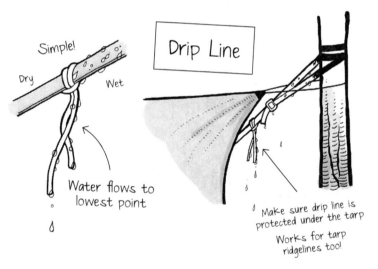

Simple!

Dry   Wet

Drip Line

Water flows to lowest point

Make sure drip line is protected under the tarp

Works for tarp ridgelines too!

GUYLINES

Diamond or a-sym tarps have as few as two guy points, so set-up can be fast. Guylines of approximately six feet allow enough length to reach nearby natural supports (rocks, branches, etc.) or stakes. In adverse conditions, bring enough guyline to pitch the tarp low for best protection, or pitch high to create a porch for better views and ventilation when the weather is calm.

Many tarps stretch during the night (especially nylon-based tarps) when moisture (e.g., dew, rain, and condensation) accumulates on the fabric, so even the tightest pitch before bed may slacken by morning.

You can create self-tensioning guylines by retrofitting the line with a piece of elastic shock cord. You can also buy self-tensioning guylines ready-made from several manufacturers. When you set the guyline, pull it tight so the shock cord is stretched out. With shock cord on the guyline, the tarp will remain taut because the shock cord takes up the slack as the fabric stretches through the night.

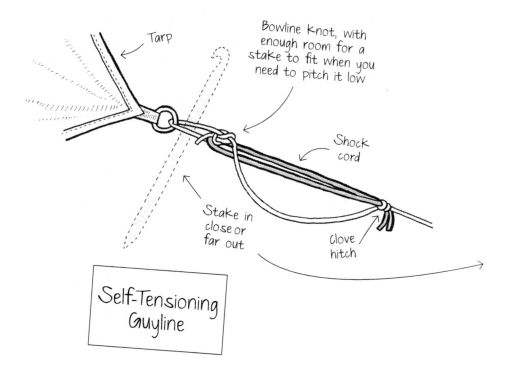

Tarp

Bowline Knot, with enough room for a stake to fit when you need to pitch it low

Shock cord

Stake in close or far out

Clove hitch

Self-Tensioning Guyline

TARP PITCHING TIPS

When I got my first camping hammock, a Hennessy, the recommendation at the time was to attach the tarp directly to the hammock suspension rope. "Brilliant!" I thought, "pitch the hammock and tarp at once!" But once I got in the hammock, the center of the tarp sagged too far and I lost the taut pitch. This isn't a problem with Hennessy Hammock, but rather a quirk with pitching the tarp to the hammock suspension. Using self-tensioning guylines and ridgeline tie-outs can help with this, but the best way is to tie the tarp directly to the tree/anchor point. Keeping the tarp tied off separately from the hammock ensures it will stay taut regardless of movement in the hammock.

IN FAIR WEATHER, a tarp may be optional, but is good to have close at hand. For this reason, string up the tarp ridgeline before going to bed, so if needed, the tarp is ready to clip on. Some hangers keep their tarp rolled up or stuffed in tube-like Snake Skin sacks so deployment is fast.

When rain isn't in the forecast but wind and dew might be an issue, pitch the tarp with the ridgeline at the same level as the tree straps. This will provide more space between the top of the tarp and the hammock to allow for better ventilation.

Depending on how the wind and moisture blow, pitch the tarp so one side is angled low and close for protection, while the other is pulled up and open. The opened end can be supported by trekking poles, sticks, or tied to a nearby tree. The result is a lean-to shelter with a porch so you don't have to sacrifice your views to stay dry.

If you have a big "winter" or rectangular tarp that you are using in good weather, just pitch the sides high (e.g., "porch mode"), tie them off, or roll them up and out of the way. A large tarp with multiple guy points provides more pitching options than a small a-sym tarp, so you can use them year-round. The downside is that large tarps are heavier and take more time to pitch correctly.

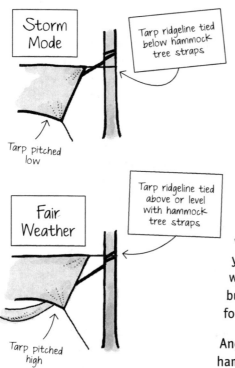

Storm Mode

Tarp ridgeline tied below hammock tree straps

Tarp pitched low

Fair Weather

Tarp ridgeline tied above or level with hammock tree straps

Tarp pitched high

IN STORMY WEATHER set up your tarp so the ridgeline is very close to the body of the hammock. Once you get into the hammock, you will drop away from the tarp. Tie it off so the end guyline or full-length ridgeline is below the hammock suspension and tree straps. When you enter the hammock, the tarp will stay low to prevent wind-blown rain from touching your gear. Larger tarps, including winter tarps, have enough fabric to button down the ends to the ground for complete coverage.

Angle the pitch on the sides of the hammock so they are steep and low to the ground. In cold, windy

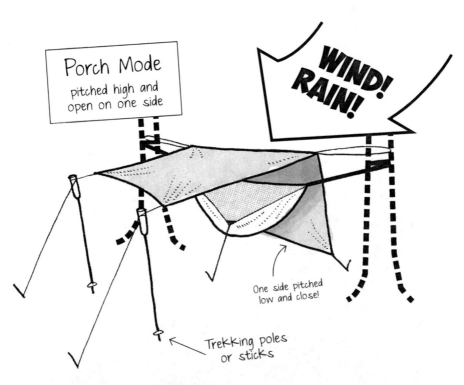

Porch Mode
pitched high and open on one side

WIND! RAIN!

One side pitched low and close!

Trekking poles or sticks

conditions, pitching the sides down to the ground can eliminate convective heat loss. A steep pitch also sheds snow better.

IN THE WINTER, however, weight and bulk are usually less of an issue because food and insulation requirements are higher. Avid winter campers often use a pull-behind sled called a *pulk* to carry the extra gear needed in the winter. A large winter tarp with multiple tie-outs, extra panels, and doors on the ends are welcome features for greater protection.

Pitching the tarp down to the snow (or the ground) traps stray heat and keeps the wind from drawing it away. In areas or conditions with lots of snow, you can build walls and tunnels to further protect your shelter or to enhance a small tarp.

It is not advisable to use space heaters, stoves, or open flames inside a tarp because the material is so flammable.

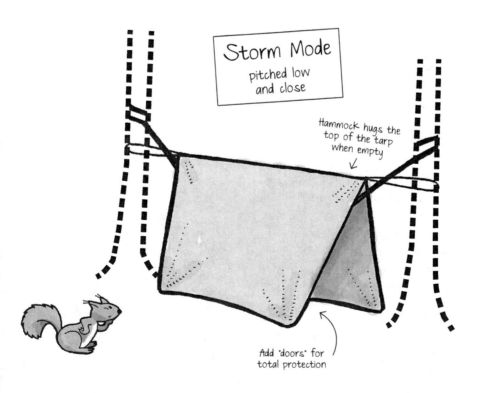

Storm Mode
pitched low
and close

Hammock hugs the top of the tarp when empty

Add "doors" for total protection

BREAKING IT DOWN
STAYING WARM

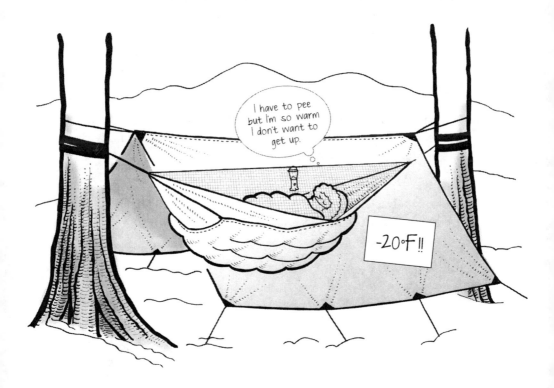

In the summer, when it is greater than 70°F (20°C) overnight, you may only need a light fleece blanket or silk sheet to stay comfortable. Below 70°F (20°C) you'll need something "extra" to stay warm in a hammock. There are many ways to insulate a hammock, so your decisions will be based on personal comfort, expense, and *panache!*

The reason hammocks stay so cool is they are suspended in the open, where circulating air (convection) robs heat from all around. This is beneficial

360° Air Circulation

Great in the heat of summer, challenging in cooler months.

in the summer, but lousy when It's cold. Since fluffy insulation is compressed when slept on, very little warmth is found with a sleeping bag alone. Warm air is trapped in the loft, or thickness, of the insulation.

Like many before me, I first used a sleeping pad to stay warm in a hammock. This method worked okay, but I found it tricky to conform the pad to the shape of the hammock, and the standard 20 in. (51 cm.) pad width didn't provide enough coverage around my shoulders. Hangers have tried just about everything to keep their shoulders and back warm, including mylar "space" blankets, bubble wrap, and even aluminized vehicle window shades.

Besides sleeping pads, hammock pioneers have tried pulling sleeping bags around a hammock, which has lead to other innovations like under quilts. These techniques have allowed hangers to sleep comfortably and warm in extreme winter conditions to temperatures below -20°F (-30°C).

WARM BELOW

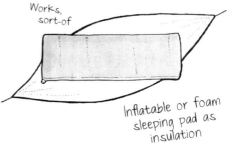

Works, sort-of

Inflatable or foam sleeping pad as insulation

SLEEPING PADS

Simple and effective, pads can be used in hammocks and can serve as a backup in the off chance you have to sleep on the ground. For those new to hammocks, sleeping pads are an easy, inexpensive option. Most camping pads are only 20 in. (51 cm.) wide, and don't cover the shoulder areas. To combat this, Dave Womble introduced the "Segmented Pad Extender" where cut portions of a closed-cell foam pad are contained in fabric sleeves, creating better coverage and keeping all the pad segments together.

Another technique that works well is to cut a closed-cell foam pad in half and turn the pieces for better shoulder coverage. One half is used for the upper torso and shoulders, and the other to cover the lower torso and legs. You can combine a short closed-cell foam pad for your shoulders and a full-length pad for torso and leg protection. Add more pads together for thicker insulation as the temperature drops.

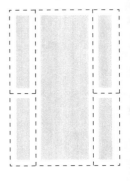

Segmented Pad Extender

Fabric sleeves to hold individual pad sections

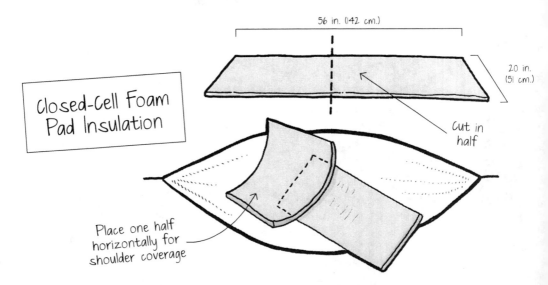

Closed-Cell Foam Pad Insulation

56 in. (142 cm.)

20 in. (51 cm.)

Cut in half

Place one half horizontally for shoulder coverage

Inflatable pads work too, but many people leave them slightly under inflated so they conform better to the hammock body. Other "pad-like" insulation options that work include Reflectix® (aluminum-covered bubble wrap used for covering duct work), vehicle window shades (the aluminum-covered style), and even cardboard.

Sleeping pads were not designed to conform to the contours of a hammock, and I've found they are not as comfortable as other options. A pad can slide around in a hammock (if not sandwiched in a sleeve), which can introduce cold spots.

INSERTS (NATURAL AND ARTIFICIAL)

Some hammocks are built with two layers of fabric creating a large sleeve that can accommodate certain types of insulation. In some models, the layers are so close together that only thin, compressed insulation, like closed-cell foam pads, can fit.

Clark Jungle Hammocks are purposely built with large baffles of fabric underneath where bulky items can be placed and used as insulation, including clothing or natural items like dead leaves or pine duff. The empty baffles create dead air space, contributing to a warm sleep.

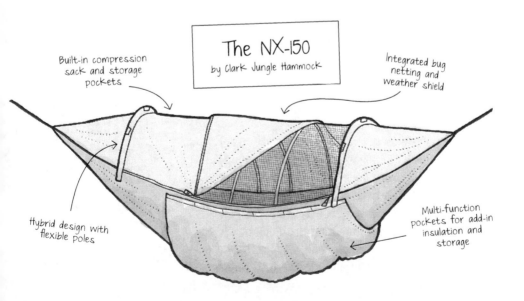

The NX-150
by Clark Jungle Hammock

Built-in compression sack and storage pockets

Integrated bug netting and weather shield

Hybrid design with flexible poles

Multi-function pockets for add-in insulation and storage

Hanging a hammock low over a pile of natural materials (leaves, duff, etc.) on the ground is another way to augment a sleep system in case of an unexpected cold snap.

PULL-OVER BAGS AND PODS

One of the earliest attempts to insulate a hammock was by pulling a regular sleeping bag around like a cocoon. A sleeping bag with a zipped foot box is needed to allow the hammock suspension lines to fit through. I used a pull-up bag like this successfully in the fall and it worked great. However, I found that I couldn't get a great diagonal lay, which caused too much shoulder squeeze. The good news is that I was warm and a lot more comfortable than if I was sleeping on the ground.

Sleeping bag pulled over the hammock

You'll need a bag with a zippered foot box to make this work!

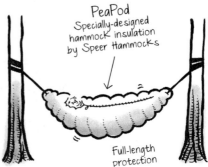

PeaPod
Specially-designed hammock insulation by Speer Hammocks

Full-length protection

An adaptation of the pull-over bag was sold by Ed Speer and is called the "PeaPod." This is a purpose-made pull-up bag with extra girth in the middle and fabric tapered near the ends. Like a pull-over bag, the PeaPod constrains the lay, but it does have additional features like a top-entry zipper that is tailored for hammocks.

UNDER QUILTS

One of the most tried-and-true methods of staying warm in a hammock is using an under quilt. There are multiple varieties available, each balancing weight, bulk, price, and ease of use. An under quilt is essentially half of a sleeping bag hung under the hammock so the insulation isn't crushed, with extra width to wrap around the shoulders. A full-length

Modified Sleeping Bag

Top quilt

Under quilt

Get rid of the zipper

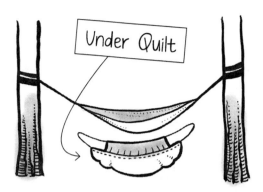

Under Quilt

Sierra Sniveller

Wearable Quilts
by Jacks 'R' Better

Drapes over
shoulders like
a serape

★ **TIP:** Make sure
your under quilt
properly seals on
the ends once it is
wrapped around
your hammock.
Precious heat
can escape if the
ends are not snug,
leading to Cold
Butt Syndrome.

under quilt was first sold by Jacks 'R' Better. Brandon Waddy later introduced a 3/4-length under quilt that covers the torso and upper legs but leaves the head and lower legs un-insulated. This is a weight-saving measure since many hangers find they need less insulation on their lower legs, where a cut-to-size closed-cell foam pad is sufficient. Wearing insulated headgear completes the system.

Just like sleeping bags, under quilts can be found with varying types of insulation (synthetic and down) and different thicknesses for all seasons. Under quilts are often made with differential baffles and designed so they can be pulled up tight against the hammock and still loft underneath, thus providing enough space to trap heat and keep you warm.

Under quilts are typically fitted with shock cords at the ends to attach to a hammock. The elastic cord prevents damage to the quilt by allowing some flexibility. Some under quilts have channels running along the edges of the quilt. This allows the quilt to slide and adjust along the length of the hammock.

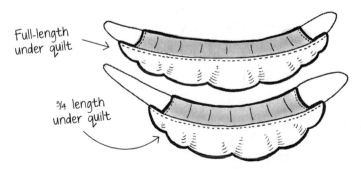

Full-length
under quilt

3/4 length
under quilt

Under quilts that have the shock cords tied off on the ends must be adjusted, sometimes with the help of a partner, to ensure it provides proper coverage.

WARM ABOVE

SLEEPING BAGS AND TOP QUILTS

Any sleeping bag can work inside a hammock, although it can be a trick getting into one. Watching a hanger wriggle around while trying to enter a sleeping bag is amusing for the observer, but frustrating for the hanger. One technique is to pull the bag around you before getting into the hammock and laying down. This works if you can easily sit down in the hammock. Sewn-in bug netting can complicate this process. Wearable sleeping bags, like the Selk'Bag, make it easy since the bag has legs and arms allowing you to maneuver and access the hammock normally.

Another technique is to unzip the sleeping bag except for the foot box. With the sleeping bag laid out, you can get in the hammock, slip your feet into the sleeping bag's foot box, then tuck the sides of the bag around you like a quilt.

In most under quilts, the shock cord makes one large loop so you can slide and adjust the front-to-back fit

The shock cord also helps keep the quilt snug to the hammock to prevent air gaps

Attaching an Under Quilt

Mini-biner

Looped over whipped end

Toggle

★ **TIP:** Improvise clips for under quilts with a stick toggle!

In fact, quilt-style sleeping bags (where the back, hood, and zipper of the bag are removed) are very common with hangers because

Sleeping Quilt

(Foot box but no back)

Perfect for hammocks!

(Or, a partially unzipped sleeping bag)

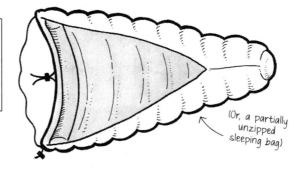

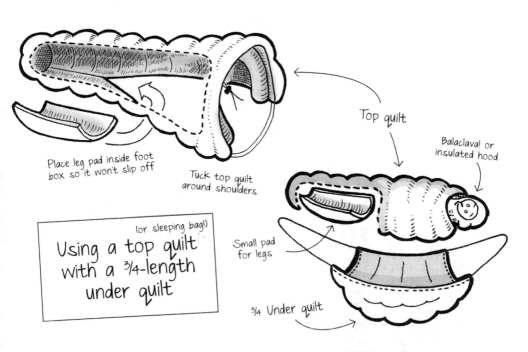

Place leg pad inside foot box so it won't slip off

Tuck top quilt around shoulders

Top quilt

Balaclava! or insulated hood

(or sleeping bag!)

Using a top quilt with a ¾-length under quilt

Small pad for legs

¾ Under quilt

they eliminate unneeded features, and reduce weight and bulk. A top quilt is a perfect match with a corresponding under quilt wrapped around the torso and shoulders.

VAPOR BARRIER LINERS (VBL)

In warm weather, 60°F (16°C) or higher, insensible and sensible perspiration (water vapor, sweat) "breathes"

through your insulation. The dew point (when water vapor turns liquid) is often somewhere outside your sleeping bag and will appear as condensation on your tarp, or sometimes on the outside lining of your bag if it doesn't completely evaporate.

In cold weather, below 30°F (-1°C), the dew point drops somewhere between your body and the outside of the sleeping bag. Tiny water droplets form inside, and over time, will collapse your insulation causing evaporative heat loss. Without a VBL, your body will work harder to generate heat, translating into sweat that may soak your warm layers and encourage dehydration, poor circulation, and low respiratory efficiency.

★ **TIP: Are VBL's necessary?** Nope. It's just another option for staying warm in a hammock. Some hangers use them in very cold conditions and swear by them, but others really dislike them.

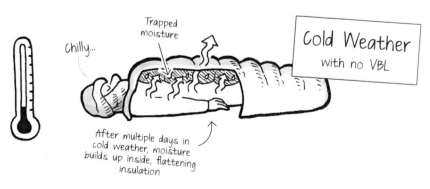

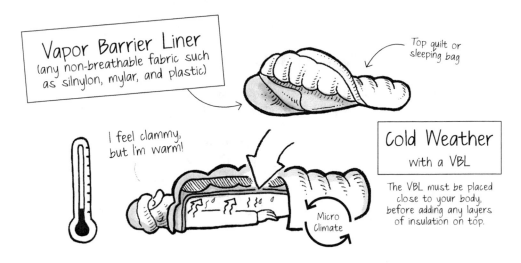

Vapor Barrier Liner
(any non-breathable fabric such as silnylon, mylar, and plastic)

Top quilt or sleeping bag

I feel clammy, but I'm warm!

Cold Weather
with a VBL

The VBL must be placed close to your body, before adding any layers of insulation on top.

Micro Climate

Your body automatically regulates to produce more or less insensible and sensible perspiration to properly heat and cool itself. A VBL stops the transmission of body vapor creating a micro-climate between the VBL and your body, reducing evaporative heat loss and overheating. The VBL also keeps moisture out of your insulation (sleeping bag, top quilt, etc.).

A base layer is typically worn between the VBL and the skin, which helps minimize the "clammy" feeling without reducing the body's natural thermo-regulation. Once your body senses the right micro-climate, it stops producing moisture.

HOT WATER BOTTLES

Another way to heat up a hammock is to boil water and place it inside a water-tight bottle, such as a 1L Nalgene wide-mouth container. Place this hot water bottle anywhere in your bag for added warmth. A good spot is between your legs where your femoral arteries are located. When I use a hot water bottle, I like it kept by my calves and feet.

On a cold February trip with the Boy Scouts in Virginia, I came ill-prepared for the conditions. I only brought a single closed-cell foam pad for bottom insulation. This was early in my hammock camping experience and I thought I'd be fine. As the temperature dropped, I began getting cold. This was the first time I used the hot water bottle technique in my hammock. The hot water bottle kept my core warm.

OTHER WARMING-UP TIPS

- **Site selection** is key. Make every attempt to set up your hammock in a protected space, away from mountain ridgelines, low depressions, water, and windy areas.
- **Dress in layers**—start with a moisture-wicking base layer close to the skin. Add insulating layers like fleece, polypropylene, or wool (wear all your clothes to bed if it is really cold!).
- **Double-up sleeping bags, liners, and quilts.** If you don't mind packing the extra weight and bulk, adding extra layers for more loft will keep you warmer.
- **Eat some food** before going to bed. Your body stays warm when metabolizing (burning) calories. Eating jumps your system into a processing mode that generates heat.
- **Drink water** before sleeping (stay hydrated). In the cold, your body is often working hard to stay warm, consuming a lot of energy. Your body continues to perspire, but the cold can make it difficult to detect. Many people don't realize how easy it is to dehydrate in the winter. When you're dehydrated, your blood volume decreases, thickens, and becomes more difficult to pump around. This is one reason your extremities (feet, hands) get cold first. Poor circulation puts you in danger of hypothermia and frostbite.
- **Go to the bathroom!** While it is important to stay hydrated, you don't want to expend your heat keeping bodily fluids warm. When you feel the urge, relieve yourself quickly—don't wait!
- **Wear a warm hat.** I like a micro-fiber balaclava or other head gear to keep my cheeks, neck, and face warm. Thicker hats or insulated down hoods are much easier to use in a hammock, especially if you use a hoodless top quilt or sleeping bag.
- **Wear socks or insulated booties** on your feet. **Wear glove liners, Wristies®, or mittens** on your hands.
- Add an **over cover, under cover,** or **weather shield**.
- Use **chemical hand warmers**.
- If using an **under quilt, make sure it is properly sealed on the ends.** Use Triangle Adapters if you have difficulty getting a good fit on your hammock (**see page 113**).

I'm snuggly and warm too

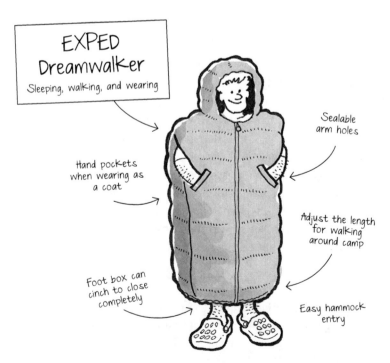

BREAKING IT DOWN
STAYING BUG FREE

Flying (and/or biting) insects are a nuisance! Mosquitoes, black flies, no-see-ums, midges, gnats, and the like can ruin any sleep in the outdoors—tent or hammock. But bugs shouldn't stop you from getting a great sleep. Most solutions for staying bug-free in tents apply equally for hammocks, although hammocks do have their own particular challenges and opportunities. Hammocks are superior to tents in probably only one area when it comes to insects: by hanging in the air, you avoid the creepy, crawly, slimy bugs that wander in or attach themselves to your shelter. Flying insects, on the other hand, are a particular problem. Not to worry! As a hammock hanger, you can take advantage of different techniques to avoid pesky flying insects.

TIMING

Many insects, particularly mosquitoes, are most active at dawn and dusk. Planning when you get in and out of your hammock may help you keep these flyers out of your shelter. Timing your trip during less buggy months is also a technique, but not always possible if your planned trip happens to coincide with peak mosquito density.

COLOR

According to several studies[1], dark colored material (clothing, fabric, etc.) attracts mosquitoes more than light colored material. If possible, select light colored hammock and tarp fabric. It is also easier to see mosquitoes (and ticks) with light-colored material.

INSECT REPELLENT

Using insect repellent, such as Permethrin, to treat the fabric of your hammock can really keep bugs away from your shelter. A properly diluted solution of Permethrin applied to a hammock can last for several trips. You can also find Permethrin in easy-to-apply spray bottles. Permethrin can be used to treat clothing, hammocks, bug netting, tarps, suspension lines—everything!

A new, natural insect repellent gaining attention is Nootkatone, a grapefruit extract. This strikes fear into mosquitoes, ticks, and other bugs and happens to be non-toxic for humans and animals. According to the FDA, Nootkatone is a food additive and is officially classed as "Generally Considered Safe." Nootkatone doesn't just repel bugs, it kills them.

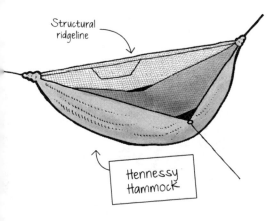

Structural ridgeline

Hennessy Hammock

SEWN-IN BUG NETTING

Several camping hammocks, including the Warbonnet *Blackbird*, Tree-to-Tree Trail Gear *Switchback*, Hennessy Hammock *Explorer*, Jacks 'R' Better *Bear Mountain Bridge Hammock*, Clark Jungle Hammock *NX 150*, and Grand Trunk *Skeeter Beeter*, have bug netting permanently attached. This is a hassle-free

1."Integrated Mosquito Management." (n.d.) http://www.entomology.wisc.edu/mosquitosite/homeremedy.html

way to stay bug free. It is very convenient to have the netting always available. Some models, like the *Switchback* and the *NX 150*, can almost completely remove the netting, or zipper it off when not needed. Other hammocks include flexible poles that push the netting out to create a roomier space inside the hammock.

If you're looking for out-of-the-box ease-of-use, then an all-in-one system with the bug netting included is the way to go.

AFTER-MARKET BUG NETTING

Many hammocks come with just the "nest," nothing more. To get bug protection, you'll need to add an extra package to your system. You can find bug nets that encircle the hammock and feature zipper entrances. These nets have an advantage over sewn-in netting because they provide coverage all around and can be completely removed when not needed.

Do-it-yourself gear manufacturers have created many bug net solutions that take advantage of a hammock's unique properties. With a fixed ridgeline, "loose" netting can be draped over a hammock or cut and sewn to fit a particular need or style.

One unique design comes from Hammock Bliss who has introduced a tarp with an integrated bug

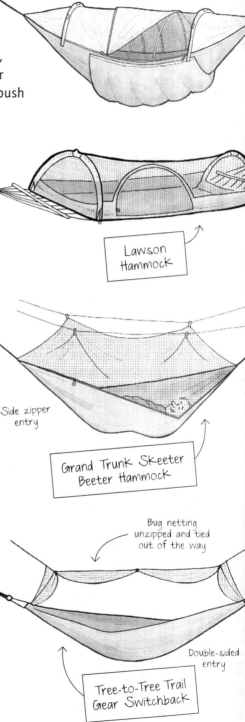

Clark Jungle Hammock NX-150

Lawson Hammock

Side zipper entry

Grand Trunk Skeeter Beeter Hammock

Bug netting unzipped and tied out of the way

Double-sided entry

Tree-to-Tree Trail Gear Switchback

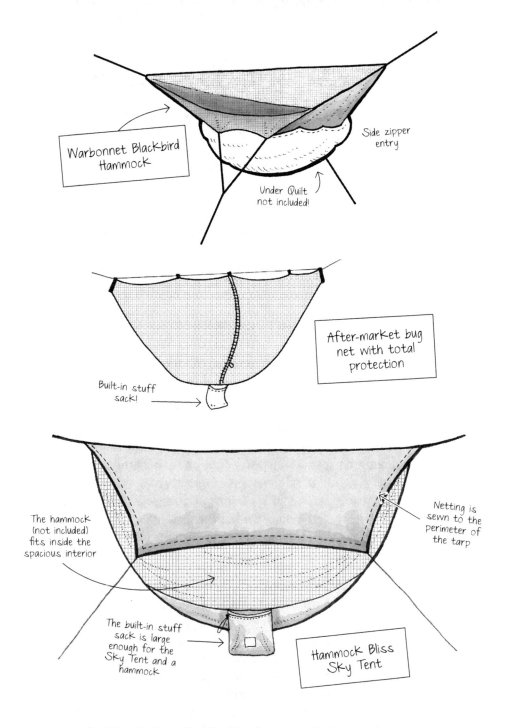

Warbonnet Blackbird Hammock

Side zipper entry

Under Quilt not included!

After-market bug net with total protection

Built-in stuff sack!

The hammock (not included) fits inside the spacious interior

Netting is sewn to the perimeter of the tarp

The built-in stuff sack is large enough for the Sky Tent and a hammock

Hammock Bliss Sky Tent

net called the *Sky Tent*. The *Sky Tent* features a bottom entry with reinforced nylon. The netting not only creates a spacious bug-free palace, it also provides a measure of protection from reflected splashing during a downpour.

HEAD NETTING AND OTHER BUG PROTECTIONS

Using a head net in a hammock is possible, but offers only minimal protection. A baseball cap can keep the netting off your face, but you'll need to keep covered elsewhere to stay bite free. I've used a bivvy bug net meant for the ground, but it was challenging in my hammock because it wrapped around me. It worked in a pinch, but it was not optimal.

One of my favorite "minimalist" bug nets is of my own design. I call it the "HUG" or "Half Bug Net." After hammock camping with my kids, I wanted a net that I could exit quickly without fumbling for time-consuming zippers or draw cords. The solution was a design that "hugs" the hammock with a simple toggle system and drapes on top for easy entry and exit. The design requires minimal sewing and is very lightweight (3–4 oz./85–113 g.). For ultra-lightweight, I've used Tulle fabric instead of no-see-um or nano-see-um netting. Tulle is less durable, but it cuts the weight by more than half.

The HUG works great on hammocks with or without ridgelines, so you don't have to dismantle or make any special modifications to your system. Simply drape or "hug" the netting over the ridgeline and secure the hook-and-loop fastener on one end. With a structural ridgeline in place, attach the shock cord directly to the ridgeline with a knot (e.g., prusik loop) or a hardware option. Without a ridgeline, simply pull the shock cord to the suspension line on the opposite side and attach. Adjust the tension of the shockcord with the cord lock toggle.

BITING THROUGH THE HAMMOCK—Some hangers have reported being bitten through a hammock even with a bug net. This typically happens when skin is in direct contact against the hammock fabric or the netting. Depending on the fabric, a mosquito can find an opening in the threads. For netting, having pull-outs and guylines on the sides can help pull the fabric away from your body. A hammock with two layers of fabric eliminates mosquito bites, as can certain types of fabric weaves. Having an under quilt or wearing clothes is also enough to protect from bites through the hammock fabric.

the HUG
"Half Bug Net"
by Derek

MATERIALS

- 2 yds. no-see-um netting, 55 in. wide or more
- 7 yds., 3/4 in. grosgrain edging (optional)
- 6 1/2 in. grosgrain toggle loops
- 12 inches of Omni tape (non-snagging hook-and-loop closure)
- 3 yds. 1/8 in shock cord
- 2 cord locks
- 2 2 × 2 in. patches of thick nylon fabric

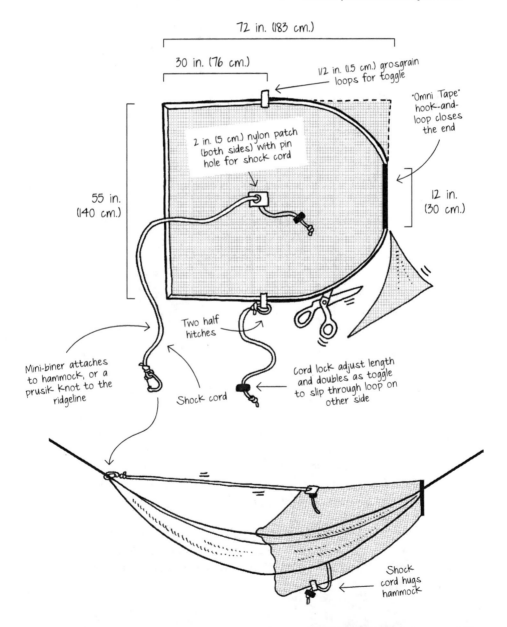

72 in. (183 cm.)

30 in. (76 cm.)

1/2 in. (1.5 cm.) grosgrain loops for toggle

"Omni Tape" hook-and-loop closes the end

2 in. (5 cm.) nylon patch (both sides) with pin hole for shock cord

55 in. (140 cm.)

12 in. (30 cm.)

Two half hitches

Cord lock adjust length and doubles as toggle to slip through loop on other side

Mini-biner attaches to hammock, or a prusik knot to the ridgeline

Shock cord

Shock cord hugs hammock

BREAKING IT DOWN
EXTRA COMFORTS & SLEEPING TIPS

Not only do hammocks have built-in comfort, are easy to set up, and are a blast to use, they're also fun to tinker with. Hangers are continuously enhancing and customizing their hammock experience. From sleeping styles to accessories, hangers are always on the lookout for the next best thing.

Many of these tips are the result of sleepless nights of trial and error, while others seem so obvious they scream, "Why didn't I think of that?" Here are some other ideas that make a hammock a superior camping shelter.

Hang your pack for easy reach!

- Use a structural ridgeline attached to your hammock to hang a gear organizer to store loose items such as flashlights, keys, or an iPod®.

- Place water bottles, books, or other items within easy reach, beneath your hammock.

- Tree webbing makes great anchor points for hammocks, but also for backpacks. Suspend packs off the ground, out of reach of salt-starved varmints who love chewing through perspiration-soaked gear.

- A scrap of Tyvek® house wrap, a small closed-cell foam "sit" pad, a contractor 3-mil. garbage bag, or a thick plastic sheet makes a great lightweight floor mat under your hammock, keeping your gear dry and giving you a foot pad when you enter/exit your loft. A pad can double as a sit pad when needed and triple as a pack frame for ultralight frameless backpacks.

RAISE YOUR LEGS

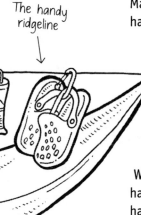

The handy ridgeline

Many veteran hangers recommend pitching your hammock so the foot end is a little higher than the head end. This can help prevent you from sliding into the middle of your hammock in the night. It can also help drain the blood from your feet if you've had a long hike. Some claim it adds a little more comfort.

GEAR LOFTS

What's better than one hammock? A second mini hammock for all your gear! You can find gear loft hammocks commercially (ENO sells them), or you can sew your own. These mini hammocks are great storage areas for backpacks, extra clothing, books, lights, boots, etc., another way to keep your gear off the ground. As always, keep scented items far from your sleeping area. Mini hammocks can also double as weather shields or pack covers for make-shift weather protection when you need it.

SLEEPING FETAL

I most often sleep on my back in a hammock, but depending on my mood, or if I can't find a sweet spot, I will sleep on my side. This fetal position is a common sleeping style and is very comfortable. (There's no trick here: just turn to your side to get comfortable). Add a pillow between your knees for added hip and lower back support.

Side Sleeping

LEG POSITIONS

With gathered-end hammocks, slight shifts in body position can make interesting changes in the composition of the hammock fabric, sometimes creating high spots, ridges, or "walls" that weren't present before. This dynamic ability of the hammock is its greatest strength: taking pressure points away while conforming to your body shape. But it can sometimes create problems. One common issue is hyper-extending one or both knees. A few leg positions can eliminate this pressure. One is to bend one leg at the knee and keep the other straight. I call this position the "ballerina." By placing the foot of the bent leg under your knee of the straight leg, you can eliminate the leg strain.

the Ballerina

Another method is to keep your legs straight and cross them one on top of the other. I use this method the most. Through the night I switch which leg is on top so I can manage any discomfort.

For flexible individuals, place the soles of your feet together with your knees apart—the frog-leg position.

LEG AND NECK SUPPORT

The hammock does a great job supporting the head, but not the neck. Personally, a pillow is too large and kinks my neck. I like to place something under the nape of my neck, akin to a travel pillow that wraps around the sides of my head for added comfort and support. A lightweight solution is to roll up any extra clothing and place it under the neck.

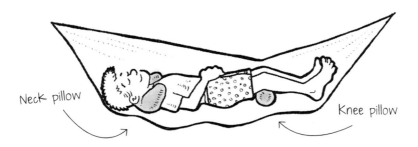

Neck pillow

Knee pillow

Many cottage manufacturers sell small hammock pillows that includes a length of shock cord and a clip so you can attach the pillow to the hammock and not lose it in the night—a feature not present with other compact backpacking pillows on the market.

If a leg gets hyperextended, try adding something under the knee for support. A rolled-up sweater or a long tube pillow adds the right amount of arch to eliminate any strain. It is also possible to adjust the hammock's pitch and sag to eliminate the "wall" under the legs. Some hammocks, like the Warbonnet *Blackbird*, solves this issue with an added "foot box" on one end so the feet drop a little more.

NO TREES? NO PROBLEM.

Even with your best planning, sometimes you'll discover that your camping spot doesn't have adequate tree or anchor support, or maybe you planned to be up above the tree line with only a hammock. No worries—a camping hammock is still well-equipped to handle these situations. If circumstances force you to the ground, your shelter system will easily convert, allowing your hammock to do double-duty as a tarp tent and bug screen—a one-person bivvy sack— depending on what you need for the night. If you carry trekking poles, you can use them as support poles for your tarp.

Above The Treeline

Use a ground sheet to protect the hammock

A camping hammock converts to a great bivvy when there are no trees.

HAMMOCK STANDS

Stands are great for backyards, especially if there are no other options for anchors nearby. Most commercial hammock stands are made for woven spreader bar hammocks and do not extend high or far enough for many camping hammocks. You can find instructions to modify or build your own hammock stand on HammockForums.net, including multi-hammock stands, that work well with camping hammocks.

I wanted a multi-hammock stand to take on camporees with the Boy Scouts and to hang in my back yard with my kids. The anchored, multi-hammock stand design fit my needs because it was easy to build, required minimal tools, used inexpensive materials (less than $40), was lightweight, and transported easily. As a bonus, one person can set it up in less than 10 minutes (faster once all the ropes are set).

Anchored Multi-Hammock Structure

MATERIALS

3	8 ft. 2x4 in. wood boards
6	3 ft. rebar stakes
300	ft. of 3/8 in. polyester rope
1	1 ft., 1/2 in. wood dowel

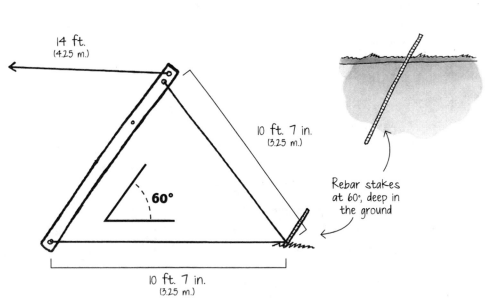

14 ft.
(4.25 m.)

10 ft. 7 in.
(3.25 m.)

60°

10 ft. 7 in.
(3.25 m.)

Rebar stakes
at 60°, deep in
the ground

CONSTRUCTION

Using an electric drill, make two 1 in. (2.5 cm.) holes on the top of each board and one 1 in. (2.5 cm.) hole at the bottom. These holes are for the ropes that hold the stand together. Next, drill a third hole (1/2 in./1.5 cm.) about six feet (1.8 m.) from the bottom for the dowel. This becomes the anchor point where you can attach a hammock and a tarp.

Each side of the top triangle is 14 ft. (4.25 m.) long. This triangle is constructed out of one continuous length of rope, with some extra length to tie the trucker's hitch—about 50 ft. (15.25 m.) total.

The side and bottom ropes are both 10 ft. 7 in. (3.25 m.) long. Cut each of these at 13 ft. (4 m.) to allow for the knots.

SET-UP

1. Arrange the stakes in a hexagon shape. The radius should be 14 ft. (4.25 m.). The easiest way to do this is to have two 14 ft. (4.25 m.) strings. From the center point, measure out the first stake point with the first string. From there, use the second string from the first stake and the string from the center point to determine the next stake point. Use this pattern to determine the six stake points.

2. Tie off the side and bottom ropes. Use two half-hitches to tie off both ends. It is important that the side ropes are individual pieces, but the bottom rope could be a continuous line about 24 ft. (7.3 m.) long that threads through the bottom hole in the pole.

3. Thread the top rope through the top holes. Pull the rope to take up the slack and the stand will rise. Tie a figure-8-on-a-bight on one end and use this as the anchor point, then tie a trucker's hitch to get the structure taut. Make any minor tweaking in the knots to ensure the posts are at a 60° angle.

Scan this QR code to watch a video of the author setting up this hammock stand!

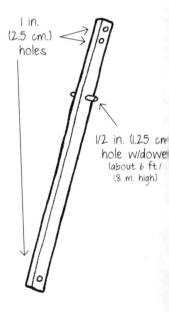

1 in. (2.5 cm.) holes

1/2 in. (1.25 cm.) hole w/dowel (about 6 ft./ 1.8 m. high)

Top detail

★ **TIP:** I purchased three 100 ft. (30 m.) lengths of rope, each a different color: Red, for the top; Yellow, for the sides; and Green for the bottom to visually organize the set-up.

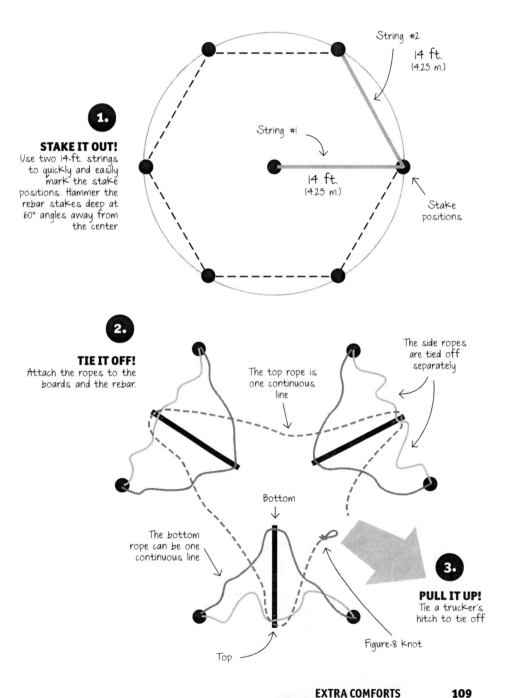

String #2
14 ft.
(4.25 m.)

String #1

14 ft.
(4.25 m.)

Stake positions

1.

STAKE IT OUT!
Use two 14-ft. strings to quickly and easily mark the stake positions. Hammer the rebar stakes deep at 60° angles away from the center

2.

TIE IT OFF!
Attach the ropes to the boards and the rebar.

The top rope is one continuous line

The side ropes are tied off separately

Bottom

The bottom rope can be one continuous line

3.

PULL IT UP!
Tie a trucker's hitch to tie off

Figure-8 Knot

Top

HANGING INDOORS

When you can't get enough hammock camping but you've run out of vacation days, It's time to set up your hammock indoors. This is a great way to test new gear and get your shelter "dialed in" before your next ultimate hang. The same rules apply to hanging indoors as outdoors (e.g., distance between anchor points, height off the ground, safety, etc.), the trouble is finding a suitable place to hang and place anchors (or getting permission to drill holes in the walls).

In my own home, I have anchor points set in two rooms where I can hang multiple hammocks. Since the wood studs are hidden behind paint and sheetrock (typically), carefully tap the walls to locate the wood (you can also use electronic "stud finders"). Use large, heavy-duty eye bolts or similar hardware to serve as anchor points. Pre-drill pilot holes, then secure the eye bolts into the wall. Now you can set up a hammock inside whenever you need a break.

More and more people are hanging indoors (some full-time!) to enjoy the benefits of hammocking close to home.

SITTING IN A HAMMOCK

Yes, there are tips for sitting in a hammock! Hammocks make great recliners, loungers, and chairs, and can even simulate big bean bags. There are various ways you can manipulate the fabric of a gathered-end hammock to suit your needs.

If you've ever sat perpendicular in a hammock, you might have experienced what I call the "bucket seat" effect. Gathered-end hammocks have this effect where you literally "fall in" to the

the Bucket Seat

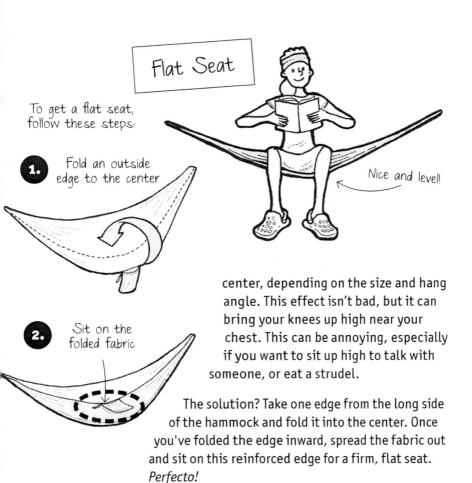

Flat Seat

To get a flat seat, follow these steps:

1. Fold an outside edge to the center

2. Sit on the folded fabric

Nice and level!

center, depending on the size and hang angle. This effect isn't bad, but it can bring your knees up high near your chest. This can be annoying, especially if you want to sit up high to talk with someone, or eat a strudel.

The solution? Take one edge from the long side of the hammock and fold it into the center. Once you've folded the edge inward, spread the fabric out and sit on this reinforced edge for a firm, flat seat. *Perfecto!*

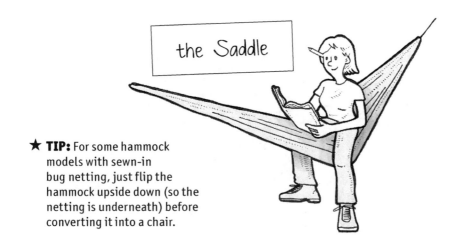

the Saddle

★ **TIP:** For some hammock models with sewn-in bug netting, just flip the hammock upside down (so the netting is underneath) before converting it into a chair.

Another popular seat position is what I call the "bureau." Once in the hammock, crisscross your legs and use the hammock's slanted fabric as a make-shift desk. With a lantern positioned overhead, it makes a great workspace to write in a journal, review a map for the next days' trek, or to prop up a good book.

the Bureau

Makes a great desk!

Hammock fabric can be moved, turned, and manipulated to create new shapes, which in turn creates new possibilities.

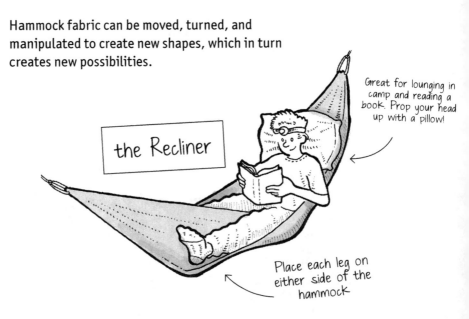

the Recliner

Great for lounging in camp and reading a book. Prop your head up with a pillow!

Place each leg on either side of the hammock

TRIANGLE ADAPTERS FOR UNDER QUILTS

Sometimes, no matter what you try, an under quilt just won't fit or adjust correctly. On some hammocks, traditional under quilt suspension can pull the quilt out too far, creating unwanted gaps. A triangle adapter moves the attachment point closer to the center of the hammock, reducing the under quilt suspension angle, helping to close the gaps and creating a tighter fit.

Arrowhead Equipment currently sells these triangle adapters online for both full- and 3/4-length under quilts.

For triangle adapters to work, you need a ridgeline attached to your hammock. This can be part of an integrated bug net or a stand-alone ridgeline installed yourself. The ridgeline adds the structure necessary for the triangle adapters to work.

The triangle adapters are adjustable by means of clips on the corners. The corner clips attach directly to the under quilt.

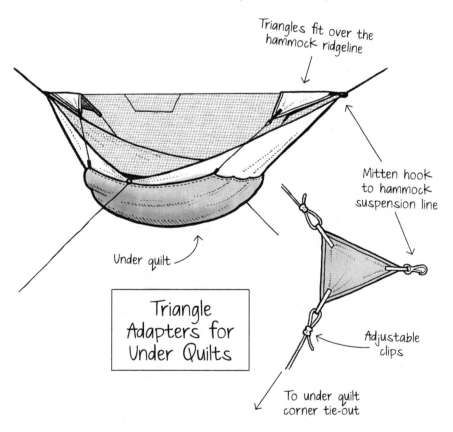

Triangles fit over the hammock ridgeline

Mitten hook to hammock suspension line

Under quilt

Triangle Adapters for Under Quilts

Adjustable clips

To under quilt corner tie-out

THE QUICK SET-UP

A well-tuned hammock system—tarp, bug netting, insulation, and all—can be set up in a matter of minutes. With good packing, quick-attach clips, and a simplified suspension line, a hammock can go up before most ground dwellers have even unpacked their tent. Try these quick steps to speed up your hang:

1. Purposefully plan and pack the hammock gear. Establish a routine that works.
2. Set the tarp
3. Attach the webbing straps
4. Suspend the hammock
5. Connect insulation (and bug net, if separate)

PLANNING AND PACKING

Planning and packing are the keys to setting up quickly and efficiently. As the saying goes, "garbage in, garbage out." If your gear is poorly packed, it will hamper a quick hang. As a general rule I keep the hammock components separate. In wet weather, my tarp stays compartmentalized outside my pack where it can be quickly accessed without disturbing anything else in my pack. As a bonus, the tarp can air out while I hike. Some people keep the hammock and insulation packed together. I keep the hammock separate so I can ensure my insulation stays dry while I set up. Then, if I'm stopping for a lunch break and need a soft chair, I can pull out the hammock and not mess with insulation or rain protection.

Many of my hammocks have built-in stuff sacks, and I carefully pack the hammocks in from the center so the two ends with the suspension line (Whoopie slings, in my case) are at the top of the sack when I'm done. In this way, I can unpack the hammock and reveal it little-by-little so it never

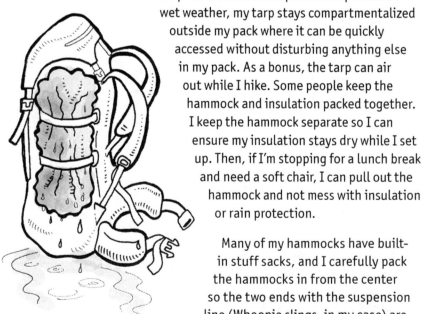

Store your wet tarp on the outside of your pack

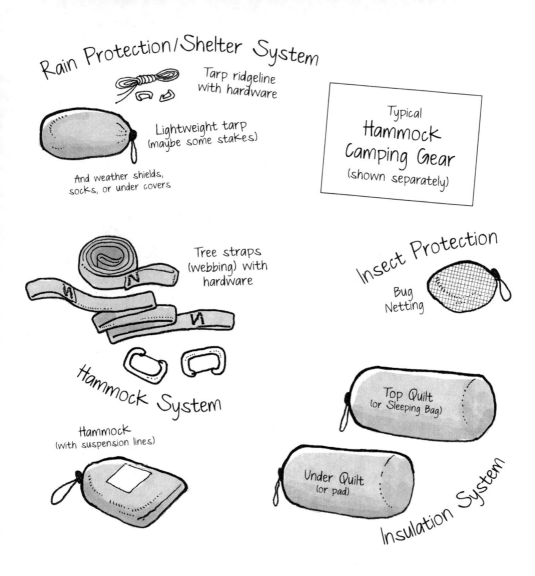

Rain Protection/Shelter System

Tarp ridgeline with hardware

Lightweight tarp (maybe some stakes)

And weather shields, socks, or under covers

Typical
Hammock Camping Gear
(shown separately)

Tree straps (webbing) with hardware

Insect Protection

Bug Netting

Hammock System

Hammock
(with suspension lines)

Top Quilt
(or Sleeping Bag)

Under Quilt
(or pad)

Insulation System

touches the ground. Tarps can be packed the same way, if you're careful, so the two ends on the ridgeline are the last to be stuffed in and the first to come out when you're ready to hang.

Long, tube-style stuff sacks called "Snake Skins" developed by Hennessy Hammock, can also be used to pack everything together. These Snake Skins remain attached to the suspension lines, so when It's time to pack up, you simply pull the tube over your sleeping system to store. Snake Skins, once stuffed, can be unwieldy, so be sure to wrap them up. I like to use the tree webbing straps to wrap up a stuffed Snake Skin sack. You can find Snake Skins in a variety of sizes: small and thin to fit a tarp, or large and wide for a complete system including tarp, insulation, and hammock kit.

Unpack

When you're ready to deploy, pull one side out at a time so the hammock never touches the ground

Pack

Stuff the hammock from the center so the two ends are the last inside

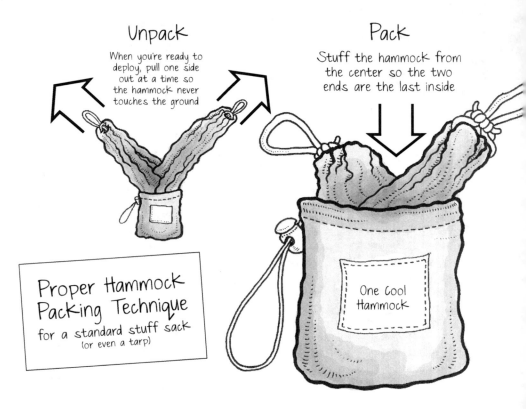

Proper Hammock Packing Technique
for a standard stuff sack
(or even a tarp)

One Cool Hammock

Suspension comes out through a button hole

Bishop Bag

The hammock comes out of a cinched opening

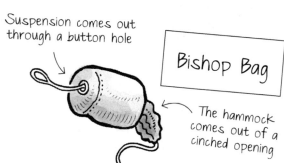

★ **TIP:** Use large Snake Skin stuff sacks if you want to pack your hammock and insulation together in this way.

Snake Skins
by Hennessy Hammock

Use the tree webbing straps to tie up the snake skin

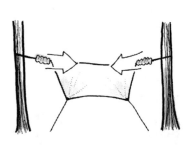
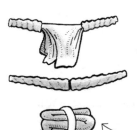

Packing Your Hammock Gear

Last In, First Out!

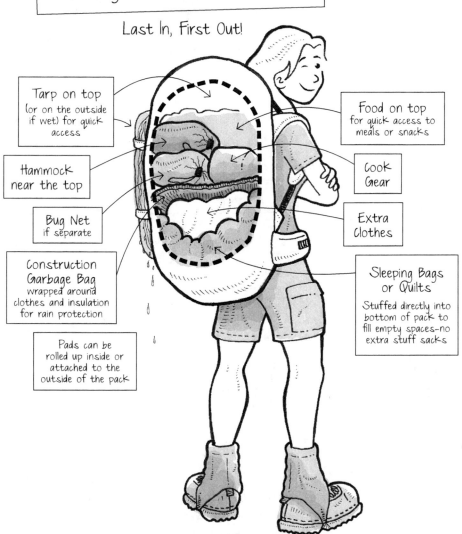

Tarp on top (or on the outside if wet) for quick access

Hammock near the top

Bug Net if separate

Construction Garbage Bag wrapped around clothes and insulation for rain protection

Pads can be rolled up inside or attached to the outside of the pack

Food on top for quick access to meals or snacks

Cook Gear

Extra Clothes

Sleeping Bags or Quilts
Stuffed directly into bottom of pack to fill empty spaces-no extra stuff sacks

Stuff sacks with a button hole on one end and a cinch lock on the other, called Bishop Bags, can also store the hammock for quick set-ups. Double-sided stuff sacks serve a similar purpose. These bags typically stay connected to the hammock suspension, like Snake Skins. You can even skip using stuff sacks all together if you want to pack your hammock kit—insulation and all—directly into your backpack. An advantage of keeping components together (e.g., the bug netting sewn or pre-attached to the hammock) is that it can speed up the set-up process. Again, find a system that works for you and practice so you can set up quickly if you're caught in the rain or in the dark.

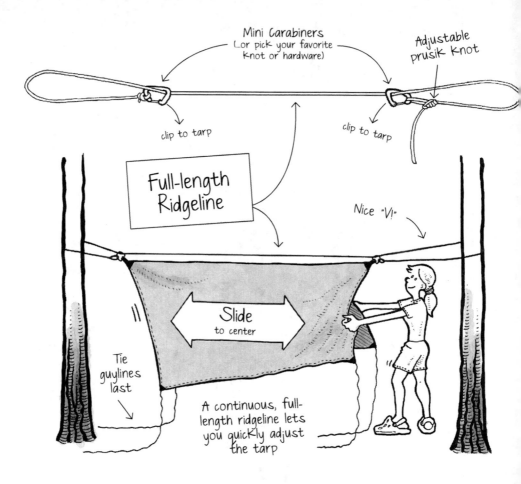

Mini Carabiners
(...or pick your favorite
knot or hardware)

Adjustable
prusik knot

clip to tarp

clip to tarp

Full-length
Ridgeline

Nice "V!"

Slide
to center

Tie
guylines
last

A continuous, full-length ridgeline lets you quickly adjust the tarp

SET THE TARP

Using the "Three Paces" method described on **page 41**, select sturdy trees the right distance apart. I like using a full-length ridgeline that is packed separately from my tarp. Two mini carabiners are attached to this ridgeline, one on a loop at the end and the other clipped to a prusik knot so it can adjust along the ridgeline depending on the tree diameter and distance between the trees. Wrap one end of the line around the tree and clip the carabiner to the line. Do the same to the other side.

With the ridgeline set, open the tarp stuff sack, pull one beak end, and clip the D-ring to the carabiner. I pack my tarp so the two ridgeline ends are near the

★ **TIP:** Set the tarp ridgeline high or low depending on weather conditions.

A Bishop Bag has a button hole on one end for the suspension line

Bishop Bag
(or double-sided stuff sack)

Hammock never touches the ground!

★ **TIP:** Speed the set-up by using hardware options like Dutch clips or carabiners. Long webbing straps like the KAMMOK Python Straps also speed the set-up with pre-sewn connection points.

top for easy recovery. This allows me to pull the tarp out and clip the other side without the tarp touching the ground.

Adjust the ridgeline so the tarp is almost taut between the trees, but loose enough that you can slide the tarp back and forth without cutting into the tree bark.

Leave the corner guylines of the tarp hanging loose to slide the tarp until it is centered between the trees. Finally, secure the tarp by tying the guylines. If you're lucky, use nearby trees or shrubbery to tie off the guylines. In areas where large rocks are common, use them instead: no stakes required.

Pitching the tarp takes only a few moments, providing a dry space to set up the rest of your gear.

If your tarp has end-only tie-outs, tie up one side, then slowly pull out the tarp and tie off the other. A taut-line hitch is a great adjustable knot, but you can also use hardware options.

NEXT, THE WEBBING AND HAMMOCK

Once the tarp is centered you can use it as a guide for your hammock. With the ridgeline, measure where to place the tree-hugging webbing straps. Reach about 1 ft. (30 cm.) above the tarp ridgeline to attach the straps around the tree. This gets the hammock suspension close to the magic 30 degree angle (**see page 43**).

To secure the webbing, I recommend quick connecting hardware. I prefer Dutch clips, which I find to be the easiest, quickest, and lightest hardware option currently available. Depending on the diameter of the tree, adjust the webbing to get the straps at the right length.

Once both anchor points are set, grab your hammock (packed in its own bag) and attach an end to one tree hugger, then slowly pull out the fabric and attach the second end to the final tree strap so it doesn't touch the ground.

Depending on your preference, you may find other options quicker or easier. Personally, I find that the right combination of hardware is always faster than lashing rope or tying knots.

LAST, INSULATION AND EXTRA GEAR

Some may argue that once the hammock is pitched, the timer stops, but since the insulation and bug netting are integral components to hammock camping, go for the gold!

Most under quilts attach by means of a mini carabiner to the ends of the hammock—another way to make

★ **TIP:** Hang Your Own Hang (HYOH). In other words: do what works for you. If you are comfortable and enjoying the experience, then stick with it!

★ **TIP:** Hammocks aren't just great for long-distance ultra-light backpackers alone, they're perfect for week-long scout camps, epic canoe or kayak trips, weekend car camping adventures, relaxing during a day hike, or taking a rest indoors.

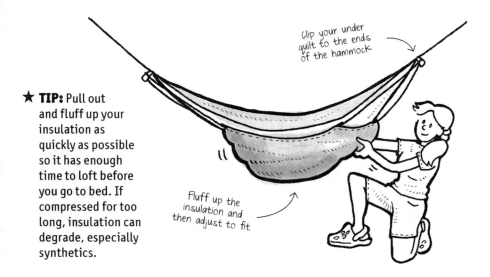

Clip your under quilt to the ends of the hammock

Fluff up the insulation and then adjust to fit

★ **TIP:** Pull out and fluff up your insulation as quickly as possible so it has enough time to loft before you go to bed. If compressed for too long, insulation can degrade, especially synthetics.

set-up quick and easy. Some under quilts work better with triangle adapters (**see page 113**) or with certain models of hammocks, and can slow down the set up unless it is pre-set. If you're using pads, place them inside your hammock and fluff up your sleeping bag or quilt to lay on top.

Finally, add any extra components like bug netting (unless your hammock comes pre-equipped), or weather covers (**see page 77**). My personal preference for bug netting is the HUG, or half bug net (**see page 101**). This minimalist netting connects quickly around my hammock and tucks into the under quilt for added protection.

PACKING OUT

When It's time to pack up, hangers have it easy. Hammock insulation can be stuffed while sitting in bed. Since I use my backpack as a large stuff sack, I can sit and stuff the top quilt and the under quilt directly into the bottom of the pack, inside a large 3-mil. contractor garbage bag. The insulation never touches the ground. I change out of my sleeping clothes and pack them next into the pack. The rest of the gear gets re-packed in reverse order as it did coming out: bug net, hammock, suspension system, cook kit, and food. The tarp is packed last. If wet, I place it in an outer mesh pocket or under the straps, otherwise it goes into the pack on the very top.

When packing the tarp, unhook one end and begin stuffing from the center. Continue packing until only the two ridgeline ends are left at the top

Easy Pack
Ready in 3½ minutes

detach this end first

1.

pack from the center

2.

pack this end last (leave it attached till the end)

3.

Contractor 3-mil garbage bag as a liner

Backpack

Stuff sleeping quilts directly into backpack, foot-end first so air can escape

STORING AND CLEANING

After a trip, it is important to take good care of your gear so it will last for a long time. Make sure the tarp is completely dry before packing to avoid mildew. The same rule applies for insulation such as sleeping bags and quilts. It may take a few days to fully air dry down and synthetic insulation.

Hammocks can be periodically machine or hand washed using mild detergents. Allow a hammock to dry before packing. Check individual care instructions for machine washing and drying.

Hammocks and tarps can safely store in a compressed stuff sack. Insulation, on the other hand, should be stored in large, breathable storage bags so the loft isn't damaged.

Wash any dirt or debris off your gear. Synthetic fabrics should not be left out in the sun for long periods to avoid ultraviolet (UV) damage.

Inspect all gear for wear and tear. Replace or repair as needed.

APPENDICES

FURTHER READING

If you want to stay on top of new innovations and chat with other hangers, there's no better place than HammockForums.net (HF). At HF, you'll find tips, techniques, lists of participating gear manufacturers, and opportunities for sweet gear deals. The folks there are friendly, helpful, and willing to exchange knowledge to help a fellow hanger. Registration is free and the conversation is always engaging.

HAMMOCK FORUMS
> www.hammockforums.net

Still can't get enough hammock camping? Me neither. There's hope! These websites have tips and techniques that will keep you mesmerized for days.

SPEER'S HAMMOCK TIPS
> www.speerhammocks.com/Tips/Tips.htm

RISK'S ULTRALIGHT HIKING
> www.imrisk.com

SGT ROCK'S HAMMOCK TIPS
> www.hikinghq.net

JUST JEFF'S HAMMOCK CAMPING
> www.tothewoods.net

GRIZZLYADAMS/PROFESSOR HAMMOCK
> www.youtube.com/user/ProfessorHammock

SHUG'S HAMMOCK 101 VIDEOS
> www.youtube.com/user/shugemery

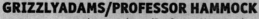

HAMMOCK RETAILERS & SUPPLIERS

While you can buy a hammock almost anywhere, I've put together a list of those manufacturers who specialize in hammock camping gear and accessories. Scan this QR code to easily connect with these manufacturers online.

theultimatehang.com

COMPANY	HAMMOCKS	TARPS	BUG NETS	SUSPENSION	INSULATION	OTHER GEAR	NOTES
2Q & ZQ Hammock Specialities www.2qzqhammockhanger.com		×	×			×	Hammock Zipper Mods
Arrowhead Equipment www.arrowheadequipment.webs.com		×		×	×	×	DIY Supplies + Custom Work
Black Rock Gear www.blackrockgear.com						×	
Byer of Maine Hammocks www.byerofmaine.com	×		×	×		×	
Clark Jungle Hammocks www.junglehammock.com	×	×	×	×	×		
Claytor Mosquito Hammocks www.mosquitohammock.com	×	×	×				
Crazy Creek www.crazycreek.com	×	×	×				
DD Hammocks www.ddhammocks.com	×	×	×	×	×	×	
DP Hammock Gear www.dphammockgear.com	×	×	×	×		×	
DutchWare dutchware.outdoortrailgear.com				×		×	DIY Supplies
Eagles Nest Outfitters (ENO) www.eaglesnestoutfittersinc.com	×	×	×	×	×	×	

Company	Hammocks	Tarps	Bug Nets	Suspension	Insulation	Other Gear	Notes
Exped (Expedition Equipment) www.exped.com	×	×	×	×		×	
Gargoyle Gear www.gargoylegear.webs.com	×	×			×	×	DIY Supplies + Custom Work
Gossamer Gear www.gossamergear.com		×			×		DIY Supplies
Grand Trunk www.grandtrunkgoods.com	×	×	×	×	×	×	
Hammock Bliss www.hammockbliss.com	×	×	×	×		×	
Hammock Gear.com www.hammockgear.com		×		×	×	×	DIY Supplies + Custom Work
Hennessy Hammock www.hennessyhammock.com	×	×	×	×	×	×	
Hyperlite Mountain Gear www.hyperlitemountaingear.com		×					
Jacks 'R' Better www.jacksrbetter.com	×	×	×	×	×	×	DIY Supplies
KAMMOK www.kammok.com	×	×	×	×	×	×	
Lawson Hammock www.lawsonhammock.com	×	×	×	×			
Leigh Lo's Under Quilts www.eighlounderquilts.webs.com					×		
Molly Mac Pack Gear www.mollymacpack.com					×	×	
Mountain Laurel Designs www.mountainlaureldesigns.com		×	×		×	×	Custom Work
MountainGoat Gear www.mountaingoathatsandgoods.com						×	
My DIY Gear by *"Papa Smurf"* www.mydiygear.com	×	×	×	×	×	×	Custom Work
New Tribe—Tree Boat Hammocks www.newtribe.com	×	×	×	×	×	×	

COMPANY	HAMMOCKS	TARPS	BUG NETS	SUSPENSION	INSULATION	OTHER GEAR	NOTES
NK Outdoors www.nkoutdoorgear.webs.com	×	×		×		×	
Outdoor Equipment Supplier www.outdoorequipmentsupplier.com		×				×	
Oware Outdoor Gear www.owareusa.com		×				×	DIY Supplies
Planet Hammock www.planethammock.nl	×	×	×	×			
Smart Outdoors www.smartoutdoors.webs.com				×		×	
SoCo Hammocks www.socohammocks.com	×			×			
Speer Hammocks www.speerhammocks.com	×	×	×	×	×	×	
Te-Wa Under Quilts www.tewaunderquilts.webs.com					×		
Terra Rosa Gear www.terrarosagear.com		×				×	Custom Work
Ticket To The Moon Hammocks www.ticketothemoon.com	×	×	×	×			
Tree to Tree Trail Gear www.tttrailgear.com	×	×	×	×	×	×	
Trek Light Gear www.treklightgear.com	×	×	×	×		×	
UK Hammocks www.ukhammocks.co.uk	×			×		×	DIY Supplies
Warbonnet Outdoors www.warbonnetoutdoors.com	×	×	×	×	×		
Whoopie Slings.com www.whoopieslings.com				×		×	Custom Work
Wilderness Logics www.wildernesslogics.com	×	×	×	×	×	×	
ZPacks www.zpacks.com		×				×	

HAMMOCK GEAR CHECKLIST

Select gear appropriate for the season and the trip (e.g., warmer sleeping bags, snow gear, etc.).
This is a generic gear checklist that should only be used as a guide.

Gear	Page(s)

SHELTER

- ❏ Hammock 44–50
  - ❏ Tree Webbing Straps 53–55
  - ❏ Suspension Lines 56–59
  - ❏ Rigging Hardware* 60–62
  - ❏ Hammock Ridgeline* 43
  - ❏ Bug Net* 96–101
  - ❏ Gear Loft* 103
  - ❏ Ridgeline Gear Organizer* 21, 29, 103
  - ❏ Floor Mat* 21, 78, 103
- ❏ Tarp. 73–76
  - ❏ Weather Cover* 77
  - ❏ Hammock Sock* 77
  - ❏ Guylines 79–80
  - ❏ Stakes* 29, 80
  - ❏ Tarp Ridgeline 71
  - ❏ Rigging Hardware* 68–73

SLEEPING

- ❏ Under Quilt. 88–90
- ❏ Top Quilt 91
- ❏ Sleeping Bag. 88, 90–93
- ❏ Sleeping Pad(s) 86, 91
- ❏ Vapor Barrier Liner* 92–93

PACKING

- ❏ Backpack. . . . 22, 103, 114, 117, 122
- ❏ Stuff Sacks. 115–116
- ❏ Pack Liner 121, 122

HYDRATION

- ❏ Water Containers (up to 4 L) . . 37, 93
- ❏ Purification Method

Gear	Page(s)

CLOTHING

- ❏ Base Layer
- ❏ Shirt(s)
- ❏ Pants/Shorts
- ❏ Torso Insulation (2 layers)
- ❏ Leg Insulation
- ❏ Rain Gear (top and bottom)
- ❏ Socks
- ❏ Shoes/Boots
- ❏ Sun Hat
- ❏ Warm Hat (balaclava) 94
- ❏ Gloves (liners and shells) 94

KITCHEN

- ❏ Stove (matches/firestarter) 37
- ❏ Fuel. 37
- ❏ Pot 37
- ❏ Spoon 37

HYGIENE

- ❏ Toothbrush, Toothpaste
- ❏ First Aid Kit
- ❏ Duct Tape (multi-use!)
- ❏ Toilet Kit (TP, wipes, wag bags, trowel)
- ❏ Sunscreen

MISCELLANEOUS

- ❏ Headlamp/Light
- ❏ Map and Compass
- ❏ Whistle
- ❏ Knife
- ❏ Sunglasses

FOOD

*Optional

QUICK REFERENCE

DISTANCE & ELEVATION

1/4 mile	=	0.4 km.
1/2 mile	=	0.8 km.
3/4 mile	=	1.2 km.
1 mile	=	1.6 km.
1 foot	=	30.5 cm.
1 inch	=	2.5 cm.
1,000 feet	=	305 m.
2,500 feet	=	762 m.
5,000 feet	=	1,524 m.
7,500 feet	=	2286 m.
10,000 feet	=	3,048 m.

Calculating a Time Control Plan

Average hiking pace on uneven terrain is about 2 MPH (3.2 KPH).

Add 1 hour for each 1,000 ft. (305 m.) of vertical elevation gained.

Travel time = (miles traveled / 2 MPH) + (Elevation Gained / 1,000)

EXAMPLE: A shelter is 5 miles away and has 500 feet elevation qain from our current position.

(5 / 2) + (500/1000) ≈ 3 Hours of hiking.

WEIGHT

1 Pound (lb.)	=	0.45 kg.
1 Kilogram (kg.)	=	2.2 lbs.

VOLUME

1 Tablespoon (Tbs.)	=	0.5 oz. / 3 Teaspoons
1 Ounce (oz.)	=	2 Tbs. / 28 g.
1 Cup	=	8 oz. / 16 Tbs.
1 Pint	=	16 oz. / 2 cups
1 Quart	=	32 oz. / 4 cups
1 Gallon	=	128 oz. / 16 c. / 3.8 L.
1 Liter (L.)	=	33.8 oz. / 4.2 cups
0.5 Liter	=	16.9 oz. / 2.1 cups

32 oz. = 1 qt. ≈ 1 L.

TEMPERATURE

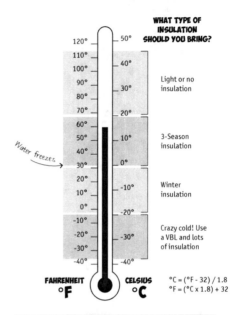

WHAT TYPE OF INSULATION SHOULD YOU BRING?

Water freezes

Light or no insulation

3-Season insulation

Winter insulation

Crazy cold! Use a VBL and lots of insulation

FAHRENHEIT °F   CELSIUS °C

°C = (°F - 32) / 1.8
°F = (°C x 1.8) + 32

PRESSURE

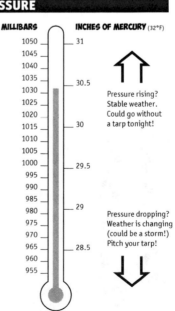

MILLIBARS   INCHES OF MERCURY (32°F)

Pressure rising? Stable weather. Could go without a tarp tonight!

Pressure dropping? Weather is changing (could be a storm!) Pitch your tarp!

HAMMOCK HANG RULER

SKY ←

Tree / Anchor Point ↑

GROUND →

Hammock →

30°

CPSIA information can be obtained at www.ICGtesting.com
Printed in the USA
LVOW08s1511300315

432576LV00003B/448/P

9 781466 263680